The RICH RICH

Tom —
May you sometime be a "member"
John

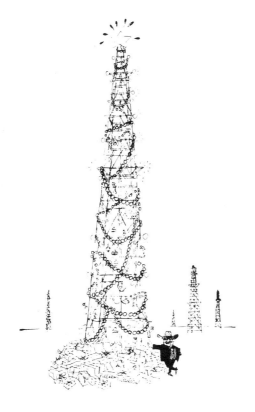

"Good heavens, Lavinia! It says here the East Wing was burned down last night."

The RICH RICH

The Story of the Big Spenders

Alan Jenkins

G. P. Putnam's Sons

NEW YORK

First American Edition 1978
Copyright © Alan Jenkins 1977

Library of Congress Catalog Card Number: 77–89624
SBN: 399–12062–9

Printed in Great Britain by
Butler & Tanner Ltd, Frome and London

Contents

1

A STATE OF MIND

'How pleasant it is to have money!' (A. H. Clough).
'Riches are for spending' (Bacon's *Essays*).
'To spend more in order to force myself to earn more' (New Year resolution of the late James Agate, British theatre critic).

*M*ost books about very rich people tell you how they made their money. This one will concentrate on how they spent it. Today we spend only needfully, not wilfully; carefully, not impulsively. We blame taxation and inflation, where we should blame the loss of our ability to take risks in a world of excessive social security; and perhaps the poverty of our desires. A climate of moral disapproval surrounds the spending of money for pleasure, ignoring the possibility that spending may have a therapeutic effect at one end, while creating employment at the other; that spending, in the right hands, can be an art. There are still a few big spenders around, and we should thank God for them: they keep money circulating, they create employment. In Texas there are a handful of people who can take advantage of the Neiman–Marcus store's offer of a $30,000 safari to Utah with a 'guaranteed dinosaur find' at the end of it; and at least one couple (no doubt on the brink of divorce) must have invested in 'His 'n' Her submarines' (once the Joneses have them, there is no point).

Wealth is a state of mind; but it is also a state of wealth. Cole Porter used to make a distinction between the rich and the *rich*-rich. He was rich, but his wife Linda Lee was rich-rich. (In Britain and America we use the unpleasant term *filthy*-rich, as in the saying: 'There's one law for the rich, and another for the filthy-rich.') The rich (like Cole Porter) may envy the rich-rich, so long as what they are really enjoying is the capacity to spend. We can thus define a true big spender as someone

7

who spends unwisely but *enjoys* it. This element of pleasure is a *sine qua non*. It is not enough to be merely rich, like J. D. Rockefeller, whose image has come down to us as a desiccated nonagenarian living on biscuits and milk while reading Ella Wheeler Wilcox; or the late penny-watching Paul Getty with his celebrated guests' pay-phone; or Picasso, who, with an estate valued at $1300 million, lived mainly on bread and cheese (poverty of desires exists at that end of the scale too).

By all means spend money on good causes, provided you do it on impulse and get a heady pleasure from it: to spend from a sense of duty or guilt, or only for tax avoidance, are disqualifications. So is a feeling of guilt *because* you spend, because *you* can afford it and someone else can't: no feeling is more socially futile than this. Arnold Bennett, all his life long, felt guilty every time he took a taxi, and on receiving a fat royalty statement from his publishers made a point of eating his next meal in a Lyons or Express Dairy tea-shop and going there by bus. One object of spending is to relax one's tensions: 'I hate money,' runs an old saw sometimes attributed to Joe Louis, 'but it soothes my nerves.' On the rare occasions when Arnold Bennett's nerves were in good order, he was capable of saying to an hotel doorman: 'Fetch me a car. A *huge* car.' That's the spirit. Near to our ideal is the spontaneous extravagance of Diamond Jim Brady, who, unlike many rich men of the Robber Baron era, decided that the time had come to enjoy himself:

'The American Beauty rose can be produced in all its splendour only by sacrificing the early buds ...' So it was, said this 1905 cartoonist, with John D. Rockefeller's competitors.

for the others, the thrill of acquiring wealth, the struggle, the chase, were what counted: too often, having made money, they did not know what to do with it. (Their children soon showed them.)

Not many gamblers qualify as true spenders (though we may make an exception of 'Bet-a-million Gates' the barbed-wire salesman). Their fortunes may be great, even outrageous, but the impulse is wrong, the spending incentive different. Gamblers take an eroto-masochistic pleasure in losing. They are motivated by an excitement which is unsatisfied by gain: they must go on until they lose. Dostoevski did this: at the moment of knowing that he had lost everything, he had an orgasm.

Some, but not all, eccentrics qualify, especially the British eccentric, who has declined in the past century because of restricted spending power. It is best if he is a Lord. The second Lord Londesborough kept his own private horse-drawn fire-engine, and loved nothing better than to leave a party in full evening dress and dash to the scene of the conflagration, the bigger the better. Gerald, Lord Berners, had a piano built into his Rolls-Royce, at a time when few people aspired to greater comforts than two carnations in a silver vase: he could not compete with David Bowie, the pop singer, who confessed recently: 'The back of my 1973 Lincoln Continental is my retreat from the world. It's got TV and pictures and plants hanging from the roof. The only thing really missing is a cat to keep me company.'

This desire for solitude brings him into the company of the late Calouste Gulbenkian, 'Mr Five Per Cent' of the oil industry, who in the 1930s spent nearly half a million pounds on laying out a landscaped 150-acre garden six miles from Deauville. Here he collected tropical trees from all over the world, and oriental birds; here a superintendent and sixty gardeners worked full-time. Gulbenkian built no house here: twice a year, staying at a local hotel, he visited his garden – to work. The public were never admitted. 'The most precious thing money can buy,' he said, 'is privacy.'

Spending inherited, especially landed, wealth is a secondary thrill, and so most dukes, Royal or otherwise, must be excluded, though we might reserve places for the 5th Duke of Portland, with his tunnels and underground ballroom at Welbeck Abbey, and Bendor, 2nd Duke of Westminster, with his charming habit of leaving jewellery under his guests' pillows. It must have been worthwhile being the 3rd Marquess of Hertford just to be able to say, as he did in 1848: 'I have a place in Wales which I have never seen, but they tell me it's very fine.

A dinner for twelve is served there every day ... The butler eats it.'
Much better to be Count Alfred Potocki, of Lançut Castle in Poland,
knowing that your estates (extending to about 360 square miles) are
bound to be overrun in any European war, and able to say without
guilt: 'We were, no doubt, a pleasure-loving people.' *His* private fire-
brigade had the advantage of being an orchestra as well, since no one
could be recruited into it who did not play an instrument.

The history of great fortunes generally goes something like this: the
first generation accumulates with savage fury, becomes tired and thinks
no further than building a monument to itself, normally an enormous
house (but sometimes a mausoleum), and securing its children against
want. The second generation has social ambitions, and spends lavishly
to gain them, sometimes by forcing its children to marry into other
rich families. The third generation, having lost the art or the need of
self-preservation, often begins to lose all. There are cases of a fortune
almost disappearing in only two generations. When E. T. Stotesbury
'the Philadelphia multimillionaire' (he preferred this official description
of himself) died in 1938 he left only $10½ million: his wealth had been
halved by the combined inroads of the 1929 Crash and taxation, but
most of it had been spent by his wife Eva and his children. It was Eva's
pleasure to be known as a giver of $5000 parties at her main residence,
the 147-room Whitemarsh Hall in Pennsylvania.

'The man who dies rich dies disgraced,' said Andrew Carnegie,
builder of America's steel industry, who gave away his millions, it has
been said, 'with no more noise than a waiter falling downstairs with
a trayful of dishes'. Giving was important to him: it was his chief way
of spending. It was important to one of Peggy Guggenheim's uncles
to build a house on the New Jersey shore that should be 'an exact copy
of the Petit Trianon at Versailles'; to another uncle, Will, showgirls
were what mattered in life: he died by no means disgraced, for he left
his entire fortune to four of them, including Miss America 1929 and
Miss Connecticut 1930, which would have been fine but for his wife's
claims and his own failure to keep an account of his expenditure, so
that in the end there was only $5229 to be divided. Adolph Lewisohn,
the copper magnate, decided that the Depression of the 1930s was the
right time to spend all he had: after his wife's death there was no holding
him, and at the age of ninety he was dancing until dawn at the enormous
parties he gave in the ballroom of 881 5th Avenue, especially on New
Year's Eve, when gatecrashers helped themselves to bottles of liquor,
some of them shouting: 'Down with filthy capitalists!'

John Pierpont Morgan – banking,
steel, shipping – and yachting (his
Columbia beat Lipton's *Shamrock* twice
in the America's Cup).

A caricature of Carnegie
distributing largesse in the
USA.

To the Maharaja of Baroda, gold and historic diamonds were important: ten gold chains, each worth £25,000, hung from the ears of his
oldest elephant. To the Maharaja of Gwalior it was electric model
trains, which ran on 250 feet of silver rails connecting the banqueting
room of his palace with the kitchen (so he was the probable inventor
of the Neiman–Marcus gravy-train which was one of the 'ultimate
gifts' for Christmas 1975). To Sir Abdullah Sassoon, who so loved his
Queen that he changed his first name to Albert, it was an endless satisfaction to be known as 1st Baronet of Kensington Gore. To certain
Mrs Astors and Mrs Vanderbilts it was worthwhile spending millions
of dollars in competition with each other, in the great days of New
York Society, to be known as *the* Mrs Astor, *the* Mrs Vanderbilt. To
Barney Barnato, who laid the foundation of his fortune in the South
African diamond rush of the 1870s, it was important always to travel
with forty boxes of cigars, even when hitch-hiking by oxcart to the

diamond fields of Kimberley: they constantly reminded him that he had escaped from the family secondhand clothes stall in Petticoat Lane, and they helped him to make friends on the way. To Alfred Krupp in 1869, wishing to build the world's ugliest mansion, the Villa Hügel, on a bare hill overlooking a river, wealth meant the power to rearrange nature. He wanted to be surrounded by trees, but being nearly sixty he could not wait for saplings to grow. So, many years before tree surgery became a profession, he transplanted a forest of full-grown trees; and such was the force of his will that they budded in their first spring.

So concerned for quality in all things was Aline de Rothschild that she asked her Paris friends if they knew of an impoverished nobleman – 'I have a vacancy for a hall porter.' So concerned for display in all things was La Païva, in the age of the *grandes horizontales*, that, in her vast Champs-Elysées house, she concentrated on the bathroom: onyx water-closet, jewel-studded taps and keyholes. It is now the Travellers' Club.

The model for irresponsible spending is probably the late Aly Khan, who after playing golf at Mougins tipped his girl caddy with a two-seater car. His father, the Aga Khan III, regarded this kind of thing as frivolous: his hobby was horseflesh ('Why should not God go racing?'), which was an investment as well as a pleasure. The families of Aga Khans are *taught* how to spend money; not so some of the Irish rich in America. 'We were never *taught* anything about money,' said Mary Jane Cuddihy of the publishing family, remembering her ecstatically happy childhood. 'We just spent it ... I can't tell you how many $500 chiffon dresses I've ruined jumping into pools at parties.' By contrast, Doris Duke's mother Nanaline, unable to forget her own early poverty, drummed economy into her daughter to such an extent that the then 'Richest Girl in the World' only began to spend, or learn to spend, when her marriage began to break up. And if her new extravagance took the form of a million-dollar Moroccan-style house in Hawaii called 'Shangri-la', who shall blame her?

Joseph Kennedy did not say in so many words that he was determined 'to spend any money to make his son the first Catholic president of this country': since Protestant Dutch often looks down on Catholic Irish, it was Eleanor Roosevelt who said it for him. Such single-mindedness is uncommon. The spending of Marshall Field III of the Chicago store family, an Old Etonian softened into his ideal of an English gentleman, was haphazard and relatively joyless until his psychoanalyst, Dr Gregory Zilboorg, took a hand: would he not enjoy his money more,

C.K.G. Billing's Horseback Dinner at Sherry's in 1903.

the good doctor suggested, if he used it in the cause of social justice? So he financed in 1940 a left-wing tabloid called *PM*, which lasted about five years, and found himself in the newspaper game up against the McCormicks.

For you can do only three basic things with money: spend it, keep and increase it, or give it away. Somewhere between these alternatives are the middle ways of 'philanthropy' (which can sometimes mean sloughing off guilt) and sensible investment in projects likely to benefit the public at large ('giving is investing' – J. D. Rockefeller Jr). One principle of giving was defined by Julius Rosenwald, president of Sears Roebuck the mail order firm, as 'giving in order to impel others to give'. Another is to be seen in foundations of all sizes (over 5200 are listed at the Foundation Library Center in New York): who, we may wonder, was the good-hearted Dr Coles who started a 'Trust Fund for Ice Cream for the Pupils of Scotch Plains and Fanwood'? Yet another, endearingly impulsive, was the lifestyle of Lady Houston, Dame of the British Empire, who from her early training in the Belle Epoque days of Paris in the 1890s had formed the habit of carrying a handbag stuffed with

13

sovereigns, and later on with £5 notes, because she liked talking to tramps, whom she would reward with money and a little screech of laughter – 'Mind you don't spend it all on drink!'

Were it within the scope of this book to examine outrageous spending throughout history, we should find that it reaches a climax just before or just after a war, a stock market crash or a revolution – witness the last days of Ancient Rome, Versailles in the eighteenth century, Britain and America in the 1920s, and the twilight of the Venetian Republic: in Venice the organization of festivals, ceremonial receptions of foreign dignitaries, ducal processions and procuratorial weddings was a state industry, employing hundreds of people, all bent on spending the state's capital, knowing that the crash must come, but not foreseeing that it would take the form of Napoleon.

But truly rich-rich spending began in America, and that is where we shall start.

2

FORTUNE BUILDERS

*P*ork and beans every meal, if you weren't too sea-sick, and a cup of water a day. This was how the FIFs (First Irish Families) of America entered the promised land, some to be quarantined for typhoid fever on Staten Island. They had travelled steerage for up to nine weeks, their twelve or fifteen dollar fares sometimes paid by the better kind of British landlord who wished to help the victims of the Hungry Forties. They came to a New York that was still a 'cow town', where wild hogs snuffled at trash-bins and stray dogs cringed in the unlighted sidestreets. One of them was Peter McDonnell, from Drumlish, Co. Longford, who became a shipping and railroad agent, earning his living from other immigrants. His son became a stock-broker and made a million dollars before marrying the daughter of another Irish millionaire, Thomas E. Murray, who was socially superior in that he was second-generation Irish and had run the Albany Water-works at the tender age of twenty-one. Within two generations the McDonnells would have racing stables, large cars, summer houses on Long Island; they would dress for their eight-course dinners; to make the Social Register might take a little longer.

Only the Irish helped the Irish, though they got on reasonably well with the Jews ('the Cohens and the Kellys'). They had to stick together and marry each other's daughters because they were Catholics, and – in New England, anyway – it was slightly worse to be an Irish Catholic than to be a Jew. However well you did, you were always an 'Irish

First glimpse of New York for nineteenth-century arrivals.

upstart' and probably a crook too. About five thousand Irish a year landed at Boston during the Hungry Forties. The utmost they could hope for was to be domestic servants. One of them, named Kennedy, ran a saloon: his granddaughters would be presented at the Court of St James, and one of his grandsons would become President of the United States.

Beans (but presumably no pork) for the Jewish immigrants, nearly all (at first) from Bavaria; such as Joseph Seligman, eldest son of the village weaver of Baiersdorf, near Nuremberg, who in 1837 escaped from the Judengasse and sailed steerage on the schooner *Telegraph* to New York. When his mother Fanny died in Baiersdorf, all his brothers came over too, William, Jesse and James. They became merchants, buying and selling anything. One of them would become a bosom friend of General Grant; another one would have President Garfield as his weekend guest; two of them would make their way by sea and mule over Panama to open stores in the Gold Rush areas of California, where you could earn $20 a day even as a bootblack. They would eventually call themselves, and in time actually become, bankers (a profession was socially better than trade), and would think of themselves as 'the American Rothschilds'; and J. & W. Seligman & Co. would be one of the issuing houses for Panama Canal stock. After their perilous mule ride nobody could be more convinced of the need for a waterway. Their high fortunes would last barely eighty years, and by the 1930s they seemed to be declining, with fewer children and too many members who though it unnecessary to work; and one or two of the present generation liked to claim distant kinship with the British Royal Family through the Messels and Lord Snowdon.

From Bavaria too came the Lehmans, settling first in Montgomery, Alabama, graduating from general merchants to cotton brokers; and Joseph Sachs, son of a saddlemaker and tutor to the daughter of a rich Würzburg goldsmith, with whom he eloped to Rotterdam. Married, they sailed to Baltimore in 1848. Marcus Goldman, in the same year, arrived in the Pennsylvania coal belt, and, after a short time as a pedlar, opened a store.

From Worms in the Rhineland in 1849 came Solomon Loeb, to the very German pork-packing city of Cincinnati. To a strict Jew 'Porkopolis' must have been a particularly unpleasant environment. However, young Solomon took a job in Abraham Kuhn's trouser-making factory, married Kuhn's sister (and Kuhn married *his* sister), so that before long they were ready to move to the respectability of New York banking and become Kuhn, Loeb & Co.

Only the Guggenheims came from Switzerland – en masse, not preceded by cautious scouts: Simon, a tailor, arrived in 1848 from Lengnau, near Zurich, with his wife and thirteen relations. They stumped around Philadelphia selling anything and everything door to door; then Simon's son Meyer invented the 'better mousetrap' – in his case a reformulated stove polish which could be used without burning your hands – and the family fortune was founded. In the next twenty years the Guggenheims made money faster than anyone except Henry Ford. At first they sold anything there was a market for – spices, linen, Swiss embroidery – and then learnt to specialize. Meyer aimed first at accumulating a million dollars for each of his seven sons. Among many experiments he had bought an interest in two lead and silver mines near Leadville, Colorado. How did you tell whether a mine was any good? Meyer didn't listen to experts: he threw stones down it, heard a plop, and concluded that there was water at the bottom. So there was: it was leaking from the Arkansas River. The thing to be, he reasoned, was neither a digger-out of ore nor a manufacturer, but a smelter: that way you minimized risk and became indispensable. The firms of M. Guggenheim's Sons (1882), a consolidation of refineries, and Guggenex (1899), an exploration company for every kind of metal the world over, showed that each Guggenheim son was well on the way to his million.

August Schönberg, who would change his name to Belmont, hoping to be thought French instead of German, was not among the ragged immigrants. He had worked for Rothschilds in Frankfurt, and arriving in New York during the financial panic of 1837, when he was twenty-one, had bought while others were selling. He was to become extremely useful to the US Treasury because he had access to Rothschild money. Otherwise he was not much liked or trusted, though his marriage to Caroline, daughter of the Commodore Matthew Perry who bullied Japan into entering the nineteenth century, did a lot for his social acceptability. No shoeless farm boy, either, was Jacob Schiff, another Frankfurter friend of the Rothschilds, who arrived in New York during

Solomon Guggenheim – one-time controller of some of the largest financial interests in the world.

the 1860s, started his own brokerage business, returned to Germany to run the Deutsche Bank, then acquired interests in the American railroad boom.

The Lewisohns, general dealers in everything from metals to ostrich feathers, filtered cautiously across the Atlantic in the 1860s from their native Hamburg. Adolph Lewisohn's fortune was made the day he saw Edison demonstrate the phonograph and was told that the telephone would be a commercial proposition very soon – and that it would need thousands of miles of copper wire. So would any gadget which had to do with electricity ... The cultured Lewisohns and Schiffs and Warburgs all knew each other, and in Germany they had numbered the poet Heine and the pianist Clara Schumann among their friends. Another graduate of the Deutsche Bank was Otto Kahn, who would one day prop up the Metropolitan Opera with two million dollars of his own money

Many of the Jews respected education, had cultural resources, even reticences, which enabled them to enjoy their money. The same cannot always be said of the White-Anglo-Saxon-German-Dutch and usually Protestant fortune-builders who have been classified sometimes as Robber Barons, sometimes as Dinosaurs. Certainly, they enjoyed their money for the power it gave them to defy the poverty in which most were nurtured; and if this was not always 'quiet enjoyment' in the legal sense it was a satisfaction which justifies the act of spending. It is usual to regard the American 'Age of the Dinosaurs' as coming just after the Civil War, when the generating of wealth by trade passed into an era of money-manipulation. There were already several hundred millionaires in the United States building huge protective shells and trying to tear each other to bits, with up to $20 million each: this at a time when, it has been pointed out, the entire contents of the US Treasury was less than $100 million. But before, or during, the Civil War had been the time when some of them had grabbed those dollars.

The classic American capitalist had to begin as a farm boy. You can't start humbler, so there's nowhere to go but up. There is very little point in being a farm boy, unless you are also a poet; and men like Jay Gould, Jim Fisk and Daniel Drew, crushing everything and everyone who stood in the way of railroads or manipulating the stock market in not yet illegalized swindles, were anything but poets. How ya gonna keep them down on the farm once they've heard of California's gold or Chicago's stockyards? Besides Civil War a century ago could be extremely profitable for men who dealt in food, weapons and cash, though only a Pittsburgh banker, Andrew Mellon's father, had the bad taste to say out loud: 'Only greenhorns enlist.'

P. A. B. Widener and G. F. Swift were butcher's boys; P. D. Armour went from farm to California gold, gold to Milwaukee grocery, grocery to meat-packing with his brother H. O.; Thomas Fortune Ryan went from Virginia farm to railroad, streetcars, electric light, coal, insurance and diamond mines (where he met up with William C. Whitney and Peter Widener) before hacking out a place for himself in the tobacco industry by attacking James Duke in 'the Great Tobacco War' in such a manner that both he and Duke made vast profits on the stock market before the American Tobacco Co. swallowed its competitors. Ryan stands apart from the Irishmen we discussed at the beginning of this chapter in that he came from Baltimore, his family had been in America since before 1700, and he only became a Catholic after his marriage.

John D. Rockefeller, a relatively well-heeled farm boy, since his father's twentieth birthday gift to him was a half-interest in a grain, hay and meat commission business in Cleveland, simply moved the business into oil: he would not drill for it or retail it, he would *transport* it – at a few cents less per barrel than his competitors, rewarding his customers by a secret rebate system. Henry Ford, son of an immigrant Michigan farmer, was forty-five before he produced the world's most popular car in 1908 – thereby speeding the departure of other farm boys from the land.

The Astors had been around since 1738, when the first John Jacob, arriving from Walldorf (one of the l's somehow dropped out), near Heidelberg, Germany, founded America's first monopoly, the American Fur Company, which stretched from the Great Lakes to the Pacific and thence to Japan and China. It was his son William who developed the family property interests to earn the soubriquet 'landlord of New York'. No newcomers, either, were the Vanderbilts, who, starting with 'Commodore' Cornelius Vanderbilt's purchase, in 1810 when he was sixteen, of a sailing boat to carry farm produce and passengers between Staten Island and New York, built a great shipping fortune and then, having hated railroads for years, switched from sea to land, finding that he had not only to join railroads but beat them as well: unable to get control of Gould and Fisk's Erie railroad, he lost millions buying up the fraudulent stock they put on the market. He survived and left $107 million.

The only great industrial family to come to America from France

Henry Ford, putting the world on wheels in 1896 with his 'quadricycle'.

Note the warning bell in front.

'Commodore' Cornelius Vanderbilt: shipping and railroads brought him $100 million.

21

were the Du Ponts, descended from Pierre Samuel du Pont de Nemours who had written *A Philosophy of the Universe* in jail during the French Revolution, in which he proclaimed that: 'No privilege exists that is not inseparably bound to a duty.' They had come to Delaware to found a colony for French refugees; they stayed to manufacture gunpowder, fight in the Civil War, and eventually make dynamite, occasionally blowing themselves up with it; then branched out into streetcars in three states, chemicals and ultimately synthetics.

Senator George Hearst, father of the publishing, acquiring and biggest-spending William Randolph, was a pioneer in California where he owned mines and ranches. He left $18 million, of which his son inherited (through his mother) $8 million and the *San Francisco Examiner*, which gave him a twenty-five-year start over the farm boys. We have, indeed, not too many farm boys left. Those who knew young Frank Woolworth in Rodman and Watertown, New York State, found him remarkable for his lack of ability to sell things at the stores where he was employed; he had a certain talent for messing about with window displays, but that wasn't salesmanship – or was it? The five-cent store idea wasn't his own, and his first attempt at it, in Utica, NY, flopped; a five-and-ten-cent store in Lanchester, Pa., succeeded and from that point young Frank plodded on to a thousand such stores in the USA and Canada before he tackled Britain. His memorials are his skyscraper and his granddaughter. His apparent dullness was partly paralleled by ex-farm boy Marshall Field I, clerk in a general store at Pittsfield, Mass., whose proprietor told Field's father: 'He'll never learn to keep store in a thousand years.' Young Field's talent was for management. Maybe the traveller in the audience at *Death of a Salesman* was right: that New England territory never was any damn good. Set young Field down in Chicago and watch the difference: he doesn't go for a safe job at Potter Palmer's store, he buys a partnership in Field, Palmer and Leiter, brings in two brothers, throws out his old partners and creates a slogan: 'The customer is always right.'

The Dukes, the Reynolds, the Dodges, the Morgans, the Stotesburys – all amassed, and (much more interesting) all spent. Their like is not often found in Britain. British Robber Barons were fewer and followed a different pattern. They seldom built palaces as their monuments, preferring to buy someone else's stately home (preferably from an impoverished aristocrat, who was likely to sell cheaper), because it was more important to move into a higher social class in an established class system than merely to be rich, and in Britain you cannot do this by ostentation alone. Thus George Hudson, the Railway King, another farm boy who by 1846, aged forty-six, controlled two fifths of all the railway mileage in Britain, was content to buy both Earl de Grey's Newby Park and the Duke of Devonshire's Londesborough Park (where he planned to build a private station) to add to his almost contiguous estates, Octon and Baldersby, all in his native Yorkshire. Why? So that he and his three sons could all become country gentlemen.

It may be that outrageous British fortunes (Sir John Ellerman, or the Guinnesses) attracted less attention than those of the American Dinosaurs because not only were they smaller, but there were certainly strong motives (such as income tax and death duties) for not drawing too much attention to them. We really do not know very much about the Guinness money and how it is spent: even the *Guinness Book of Records* does not enlighten us, confining itself to the observation that 'the greatest will proved in Ireland was that of the 1st Earl of Iveagh (1847–1927), who left £13,486,146'. We know almost nothing about the late Sir John Ellerman, the shipping magnate, who, it was always said in Fleet Street, actually employed a public relations officer to keep his name *out* of the press. Of the Marks and Sieff families of Marks and Spencers we know little but their benefactions, and perhaps they are all there is to know. Just once in a while (but not very often since the First World War) a real spender hits the headlines. It might be Sir Thomas Lipton, who, with his flair for advertising, had every reason for wishing his expenditure to be known; Horatio Bottomley, with his champagne breakfasts, which even his intermittent bankruptcies did not preclude; or Barney Barnato, who by the age of forty was believed to be earning £5 a minute. It is, after all, the spending that counts; and just as Lipton had no difficulty in keeping up with the Prince of Wales, even when he became Edward VII, so Barney Barnato, chasing the elusive knighthood, took for his royal milieu the City of London, was given a banquet by the Lord Mayor in 1895, and lavished his money on huge dinners for stockbrokers and diamond merchants and their wives. A rarity among British fortune-builders, he built his palace in Park Lane, buying the site from the Duke of Westminster.

Gordon Selfridge, completely identifying himself with English life, but retaining his American passport, was a true spender, so much so that his fortune was largely dissipated in his lifetime. 'Profits,' he said many times, graciously waving his tail like Kipling's Mother Jaguar, 'are not the only prize.' Beginning in a fairly traditional way (delivering newspapers and bread at the age of eleven in his home town of Ripon,

ALICK. P.F. RITCHIE.

Wisconsin), he was forty-nine when he sold out his interest in Marshall Field's store in Chicago before coming to London in 1905 to found his temple of commerce in Oxford Street.

The Rothschilds, spreading out from a house with a red shield on it in the ghetto of Frankfurt-am-Main, to Vienna, to London, to Paris, to almost everywhere, worked and accumulated; most loved learning, and those that spent, spent for enjoyment. Taking a peek at Alfred Rothschild's petty cash book in his New Court office in the City of London, we may note such items of comfort as a mink footwarmer (well, they had little central heating in the 1890s) and an entry by his clerk: 'Mr Alfred's weekend spending money – £1000 in cash.' And if it was true that the British Rothschilds after 1918 were 'down to their last millions', we shall see that these things were comparative.

Another Mr Alfred was Alfred Krupp, to whom the sound of a drop-forge was 'music more exquisite than all the world's violins', so exquisite that he could not bear to be out of earshot. He was one of several *Schlotbarone* ('smoke-stack barons') – August Thyssen was another – produced by the industrial revolution, who took over from the old German landed aristocracy in the Ruhr. Few of the Krupps ever learnt how to spend for pleasure. If you had asked Alfred Krupp what was the most worthwhile expenditure of his life, he would probably have replied: 'The money I invested in producing the world's biggest cast-iron ingot, for which I was awarded a medal at the Crystal Palace.' It had weighed 4300 lb.

'Deep spiritual fervour with a highly-developed business sense' is the outstanding virtue of the Aga Khans, the latest of whom, Karim, is not slow to point out that: 'The Prophet too was a business man.' Descended from Mohammed's son-in-law, the family is responsible for a financial and industrial empire worth about $300 million, embracing Pakistan, Africa, France, Sardinia and Ireland (horses, of course). With certain exceptions, the family has always been adept at combining pleasure with business.

Even longer is the tradition of the Sassoons, merchant princes from Mesopotamia, the Jews' second home after they were exiled by Nebuchadnezzar. If the Aga Khans were descended from the Prophet, then the Sassoons could trace their lineage back to King David, 1600 years earlier. Having bought exceptional privileges from the Caliph of Bagdad, in the flourishing times that followed the coming of Islam, they traded by caravan and ship as far away as Singapore and Java; and so it was for a thousand years. Then, as persecution followed the decline

Gordon Selfridge – a shop or a 'bloody Greek temple'?

of Bagdad in the eighteenth century, David Sassoon led a new diaspora to Bushire in Persia, where he raised the money to start an export-import business in booming Bombay. Other Sassoons went to Sydney, New South Wales. The sons of David Sassoon opened up a textiles and opium trade in Shanghai and Hong Kong, and were soon in Japan; and their interests now embraced dried fruits, metals, tea, gold, silk and spices. Since it was then perfectly legal to trade in opium, it is permissible to say that the Sassoon fortune was largely founded on it. After the Indian Mutiny, the first Sassoon to wear Western clothes came to London. He was Sassoon D. Sassoon, he was twenty-six and fanatically loyal to the Queen Empress, and he joined the Establishment straight away by buying a Tudor stately home at Ashley Park, Surrey.

The shipowning Greeks also love long traditions, and the late Aristotle Onassis once wanted to buy the island of Ithaca because it was the home of Odysseus. (Skorpios was only the next best thing.) It could be said that the Greek millionaires consolidate and survive, are not among the freest spenders at all; but we know so much less about them than about those whose spending is not balanced by accumulating. Secret as the Mafia, despising those of their fraternity who attract world publicity (and this means Onassis and Niarchos), they build houses and buy yachts and islands, and marry each other's daughters. Why yearn to possess the widow of an American President, whose spending is likely to astonish even you, when you can marry an even more beautiful and somewhat younger girl whose father could one day be your partner in a merger?

Onassis, son of a prosperous tobacco merchant in Smyrna, wanted to go to Oxford. Had he been able to do so, we can perhaps imagine him reading Greats at the feet of Gilbert Murray. Instead, he found himself, at sixteen, embroiled in the Greco-Turkish War of 1922, bribing the Turks to release his parents. Sailing to the Argentine, already speaking six languages, he became a night telephonist; then he set up as an importer of Balkan tobacco and in two years made $100,000. At twenty-two he was Greek Consul-General in Buenos Aires; at twenty-five, a dollar millionaire. In 1931 he bought six old Canadian ships for $125,000. Foreseeing an age of big oil tankers, he built his first, *Ariston*, in Sweden (no other Greek had done this); and then two more. By 1953 he had a fortune of more than £100 million. He was ready to spend, and to try to capture the youth he had never had.

3

CHAMPAGNE WITH EVERYTHING

*I*n mid–nineteenth–century New York, hostesses were becoming seriously concerned about 'bad form'. Was it really *bon ton* to wear a straw hat with a swallowtail coat? Was it really the thing when President Lincoln allowed men to attend meetings and social functions in shirtsleeves? Manners had improved since the early 1800s, when the original John Jacob Astor was said to have eaten both peas *and* ice-cream with a knife. But there was still a great deal of spitting and tobacco-chewing, and men in their cups were apt to fight duels. Wives murmured to their husbands: 'Dear, the Prince of Wales *never* uses a toothpick at table.' The manners of August Belmont, the banker, who had been financial adviser to Lincoln during the Civil War, were not acceptable to all hostesses: for one thing, he thought it smart to be two or even three hours late for dinner; and for another, his reputation with women was a possible reason why, in a duel, he had been shot in the thigh. He was an authority on horses, and with his friend Leonard Jerome, Winston Churchill's maternal grandfather, founded the Jerome Park Racetrack and the Westchester Polo Club. His 5th Avenue house at 18th Street was for some time more splendid than anyone else's: it was the first house in New York to have its own art gallery with north lighting from the ceiling; and if that light fell upon nudes of the school of Bouguereau, the ladies could always retire.

August Belmont rendered one important service to *nouveau riche*

New York society: at his dinner parties, 200 guests sat down to what we now call gourmet food. Not mere *quantities* of food: it was normal among the well-to-do of New York and London to serve seven or eight courses at dinner, and if you had arrived on the wrong night you would have found the family eating much the same as at a dinner party. Perhaps not caviare *every* evening; but the menu would be likely to include such stand-bys as canvas-back duck, Maryland terrapin, pâté, pheasant; and before bed, if you were staying the night, there would be squab or quail on toast, potatoes and perhaps hot oysters. The difference at August Belmont's was the wine. He did not, like William Seligman, of a rival banking house, produce nine wines to go with seven courses, which meant having two different sherries with the soup. No one spent more lavishly on wine. It was not the eternal magnums of champagne with everything that you got at so many rich men's houses, but European wines of often unappreciated vintages. Belmont knew how to spend. It was a scurvy trick of fate that he should live opposite James Lenox, learned bibliophile and philanthropist. It is said that Mr Lenox died of shock on hearing that his neighbour spent $20,000 a month on wine.

The status symbols of all the new rich in these years were the great house, the huge yacht, and (a little later) the private railroad car. The status activity was competitive entertaining. The badge was often jewellery, sometimes used in the strangest ways.

With houses, how great is great? The Astors built French châteaux on the eastern edge of Central Park. The Vanderbilts built palaces of various designs on 5th Avenue, which in the nineteenth century was still mainly residential: much was torn town in 1927 when the Avenue was widened. Along 5th Avenue, numbers 459, 640, 660, 680 and 684 were all occupied by Vanderbilts. But when we speak of 'Vanderbilt Palace', we mean of course 640 5th Avenue, the brownstone Renaissance pile built by the Commodore's grandson. A team of more than 600 builders, European sculptors and woodcarvers (there were 250 of them) had worked for eighteen months to produce a palace which, the architects claimed, was built to last a thousand years. The ballroom, typical of the desire of the American very rich to identify themselves with the Sun King, was a replica of Versailles, with mirrors, red velvet and gilded woodwork. You entered the vestibule through huge bronze doors called 'The Gates of Paradise'. Originally made in Italy for the Prince of Donato, they cost $25,000, and their ten panels pictured the Wonders of Heaven as described in the Old Testament. Once inside, you walked among alabaster pillars, walls of Caen marble, and ornaments of unthinkable costliness: one green malachite vase, more than eight feet high, came from the Winter Palace at St Petersburg. Something of this now demolished castle has been preserved in the film of *Gone with the Wind*; for Rhett Butler's mansion, the fruit of his Civil War profiteering, was based on old photographs of 640 5th Avenue, and transferred to the South, and Paramount Studios bought its carved panelling and mirrors and some of the contents of its fifty-eight rooms when, with the decline of the Vanderbilt fortunes, '640' was torn down in 1947. The Grand Hall or *atrium*, in the centre, rose like that of an Italian palazzo to the roof, four floors above, sustained by marble columns of the same height. (You get something of the atmosphere when you enter the Reform Club in London, if you mentally obliterate all the busts of Liberal statesmen.) The banisters of the main staircase ended in a life-size nude statue of a female slave wearing a tiara of electric lights (the Reform Club unfortunately has nothing like this). Electric light was the latest thing – Alice, wife of Cornelius Vanderbilt II, had presided at one of her own fancy dress balls as an electric light.

Drawing rooms, balconies, conservatories, led off the main *atrium*. They were crammed with gilded marble, mosaic friezes, statues, carvings, oriental rugs, tapestries representing classical legends, horsehair sofas, Japanese lacquer, books too beautiful to read, a drinking cup that had once belonged to Stephen Bathory, sixteenth-century king of Poland and Transylvania; and William Henry Vanderbilt's art collection, which reflected faithfully his own taste: Bouguereau (but no nudes), Meissonier, Millet and (his favourite of all) a painting of oxen ploughing, because it reminded him of the family farm on Staten Island.

'640' has now gone with the wind; but 'The Breakers', built by the Commodore's grandson Cornelius II and his formidable wife Alice at Newport, Rhode Island, as a 'summer cottage', survives as a stately home visited by gaping tourists. Cottage and contents together cost $11 million. Cornelius II, that shrewd banker and investor, did indeed endow hospitals, art galleries, churches and Yale University, but 'The Breakers' is his monument. It has seventy rooms, a billiards room in green marble and a hall forty-five feet high. It was surrounded by a wrought-iron fence which cost $5000 a year to paint. The front door weighs seventy tons, and in the countless bathrooms guests could choose between fresh water and sea water.

It had started as a three-storey brick and wood house with stables, set in eleven acres, which Cornelius II had bought in 1885 and extended.

There was a cottage for the children, who had their own butler and French chef who gave the three daughters cooking lessons. In November 1892 the house was burnt to the ground. Cornelius and Alice Vanderbilt determined never again to have a house in which wood was used. They therefore commissioned Richard Morris Hunt, an architect who specialized in French châteaux and Italian palazzi, to design (with Alice's help) a new one. Hunt had already built 660 5th Avenue and a tomb for the Commodore, and was working on a château for Cornelius II's brother, George Washington Vanderbilt.

Newport can be wet and windy, so there was no point in having the traditional central courtyard of an Italian villa, open to the sky. Instead, the ingenious Hunt (with Alice's help) put a roof over it, painting on the ceiling a *trompe l'oeil*, blue sky with scudding white clouds. Thirty-three of the seventy rooms were for staff and servants, who were all crushed together on the top floor. European stately homes were ransacked for antique chimney-pieces and *objets d'art*, and the Vanderbilt emblems (their coat of arms had been invented by Alva), lions and oak-leaves, were everywhere. 'The Breakers' was two years a-building, and had so much of Alice in it that she was called Alice-of-The-Breakers.

Cornelius II's brother William Kissam Vanderbilt also had a formidable wife, Alva. Left to himself William K. might have been content to indulge his love of horses, yachts and the society round; but Alva and Alice were already conducting their lifelong struggle for the title of '*the* Mrs Vanderbilt'. Thus if Alva had a $2 million Gothic mansion at the intersection of 5th Avenue and 53rd Street, Alice must have a $5 million palace, also on 5th Avenue but between 57th and 58th Streets. If Alice had 'The Breakers', Alva must have a 'cottage' all of white marble (even the driveway was of white marble) inspired, it would seem, by the Temple of the Sun at Baalbek.

William K. also had a little place in the country called 'Idle Hour' on Long Island, a blend of French and Jacobean influences, with 110 rooms and 45 bathrooms, an interesting mixture of period fireplaces, a cloister and a palm garden. Inside, there were gorgeous tapestries; outside, not quite in style, gargoyles stuck out everywhere.

Another brother George Washington Vanderbilt was, untypically for this family, interested in farming and forestry. He bought 130,000 acres near Asheville, North Carolina, and spent $3 million on building a château-style country house which he called 'Biltmore'. Like the Vanderbilt house at 660 5th Avenue, it took for its model the Château de Blois, adding a Norman banqueting hall. Here he employed, it was

Above 'Vanderbilt Palace' – the drawing room of W.H. Vanderbilt's house on the north-west corner of Fifth Avenue and 51st Street. *Below* Alice Vanderbilt called this her 'summer cottage' – 'The Breakers', overlooking the celebrated Cliff Walk at Newport, Rhode Island.

said, more people than the US Department of Agriculture, and looked after them well with their own shops, church, hospital and schools. His pedigree cows and pigs won prizes everywhere. He founded a school of forestry and experimented with scientific farming. One of the few educated Vanderbilts, he spoke eight languages. When he died in 1914 at the age of only fifty-two, he had enjoyed his life and left only $929,740, which looked pretty silly beside the Commodore's $107 million and his son William's $200 million. As for Biltmore, it was, for its size, tasteful: there were forty main bedrooms (we exclude the servants' quarters), and a magnificent library of 250,000 books. The drawing room, all of oak, was full of engravings; the Palm Court was full of statues; the banqueting hall was full of Gobelin tapestries; the Print Room was full of Dürer etchings, and if you happened to remark on the handsome chess set there displayed, George would reply: 'Oh, that was Napoleon's.'

Shortly before his death in 1885, William Henry Vanderbilt had an enormous book ($2\frac{1}{2}$ by 4 feet) published in fifteen volumes, all about 640 5th Avenue, containing etchings, photographs and hand-coloured drawings so that people could see the splendour in which he lived without his having to invite them in. It was quite usual to do this – other rich men, such as Louis Tiffany, son of the jeweller and the first modern interior decorator, had done the same. (Before Tiffany, it was said, most interior decoration had been done by 'gifted gasfitters'.) William Henry's brother George would have thought it tasteless, on a par with the 'rubberneck wagons', the old 5th Avenue stagecoaches with outside seats which in the 1890s took tourists to look at the exteriors of the houses of the very rich. But William Henry's own contribution to the book made it clear that he regarded his own house as free from showiness (by this he meant that it contained nothing so vulgar as a zoo or a bowling alley): it was, he claimed, 'as sincere a house as exists anywhere'. The book opened with an etching by an artist named Marcel Lancelot, whose own comment was implicit. The Vanderbilts had made their millions from railroads, and so Lancelot drew a locomotive coming out of a tunnel, surrounded by cherubs and Nubian boys carrying gifts of fruit and candy. One cherub bore in his chubby fist a bottle clearly labelled GIN.

When, in the early 1900s, Henry M. Flagler, with Standard Oil money, began the development of Florida which would explode in the boom of the 1920s, he built himself a house called 'Whitehall' at Palm Beach. Bronze doors, gold taps in bathrooms, sixteen guest apartments, tapestries, oriental rugs, crystal chandeliers – nothing new here; yet stay – a 4000 square feet foyer, marble, yes, but in *seven* shades! – and decorated with frescoes representing the fortunes of Harry Flagler: Knowledge, Happiness, Prosperity. For $4,200,000 Charles Schwab, President of Carnegie Steel, in 1905 built a house on Riverside Drive with the usual Carrara marble even in his private chapel, where the altar looked as cold as a mortuary. Seventy-five rooms, forty baths, swimming pool, gymnasium – and, the very latest amenity, bowling alleys.

In Washington, DC the Walsh family built 2020 Massachusetts Avenue, with a modest sixty rooms and a 'well' staircase four floors deep ascending through galleries to a stained-glass dome. The main staircase was lined with marble nymphs, there was a theatre, and – unique feature – a throne room. Tom Walsh, who had struck it rich at the celebrated Camp Bird goldmine in Colorado, was one of the Irish who had *not* hung around in Boston. A multimillionaire, he had gone into Washington real estate, and then to Paris, France: he was one of the US Commissioners sent in 1899 by President McKinley to the Paris Exposition. In Paris he became known for his dinner parties at the Ritz, where he somehow got to know King Leopold of the Belgians. Well, it never hurts to have a king on the board, so Tom made Leopold a grateful partner in the mine. Some day, who knows?, Leopold might come to America: naturally he must be Tom Walsh's guest, and a king has to have a throne. So the Walsh palace must contain a throne room, with a throne which, when not required, could be out of sight. This reasoning produced a *hydraulic* throne which, at the touch of a button, rose out of the floor like the mighty Wurlitzer cinema organs of thirty years later.

A yacht, in the rich-rich sense of the word, is a floating palace, and often costs nearly as much. It is not absolutely necessary that it should sail anywhere. Commodore Vanderbilt, a genuine sea-faring, or at least a Staten Island-faring man, had a yacht 270 feet long which weighed 2300 tons, as well it might, since it had a marble dining room, saloons lined with rosewood, plush everywhere, and a bathroom about half the length of the deck. Arthur Curtiss James, the copper magnate, also called himself Commodore, a title which he more than justified by sailing his three-masted steam yacht *Aloha* round the world and by being the only member of the New York Yacht Club to hold a master navigator's certificate. John Pierpont Morgan the banker had *four* yachts at various times, all called *Corsair*, presumably because he claimed descent from Henry Morgan the pirate. No denying it, steam yachts were fashionable at the turn of the century; and so Boni de Castellane, the impecunious French Count whose marriage to Jay Gould's daughter Anna put uncountable millions at his disposal, had to have one too: his 1600-ton *Valhalla* had eight officers, a crew of ninety and a staff of valets, manicurists and maids, beside the usual ship's company.

J.P. Morgan Jr., who financed the Allies in World War I (and of course was much concerned with Reparations afterwards), caricatured in *Vanity Fair* as a cut-out doll.

Since wealth confers the ability to act out fantasies, somebody, sooner or later, was bound to want the biggest steam yacht in the world. The first claimant was William K. Vanderbilt, who in 1886 built an ocean-going one, designed to cross the Atlantic at 12 or even 15 knots. Built by Harland & Hollingsworth of Wilmington, Delaware, it was 285 feet long, cost half a million dollars to build and $5000 a month to run. The decks were of teak, the interior panelling of teak and mahogany. William K.'s own quarters comprised nine rooms and a nursery: there were besides seven staterooms for guests, all with private bathrooms. The ship's officers also had private bathrooms. There was a crew of fifty-three, led by Captain Morrison, an ex-liner skipper, including a surgeon and a mechanic to look after the ice-cream machine. The ship was named *Alva*, and the launching (with American champagne) was performed by Mrs Yznaga, Alva's sister. Hardly had she said 'I christen thee *Alva*' when the ship rushed down the slipway and buried its nose in the mud. Worse things were to happen at sea – *Alva*, it seems, pitched and rolled terribly – and the ship was probably a major cause of the rift between Alva and her husband which ended in divorce.

Much more disastrous was 'the world's biggest yacht' devised by Ned Green, spending son of Hetty Green who had made a fortune out of whaling and Wall Street. (Ned liked to be called Colonel, not Commodore, and travelled about with a suitcase full of bills of very large denominations up to $10,000.) He spent a million dollars on buying the *United States*, a passenger boat which had seen service on the Great Lakes. A fine boat, but in his opinion not long enough; so he cut it in half and put a new piece in the middle. Its main cabin was Jacobean in style with a roaring fire in the open hearth, and there were nine state-rooms with private baths. He made do with only seventy-one crew, but for some reason the extended vessel needed two captains: had it ever sailed anywhere, they would have been arguing all the time. But it didn't. For it was 1916, America would shortly enter the World War, and there was a shortage of coal. The *United States* needed 660 tons a year just for hot water and heating. Everybody except the insurers was rather relieved when the boat, for unexplained reasons, sank near Ned's house at Buzzards Bay, Massachusetts.

Many were the yachts of the Vanderbilts; but one more deserves mention, if only because it was one of the last flings of William K. Vanderbilt II. In 1931 he built a yacht that was ideal for his way of

All J.P. Morgan's yachts were called *Corsair*. This is *Corsair I*. *Corsair II* became the *Gloucester* and was used in the Spanish–American War.

life, which, we have seen, now consisted largely of collecting marine specimens. He called it, in the family tradition, *Alva* after his mother. He was now fifty-three and a little sluggish, and so the vessel's second most important feature was its gymnasium, which had two exercise bicycles, an electric horse which jogged the pounds off his weight, rowing machines and punchballs. The equipment which made it different from everyone else's yacht was a seaplane, believed to have cost nearly $60,000, on its deck. The staterooms were nine feet high, the main living room fifteen feet high, dimensions to make a naval architect squirm. Theoretically designed for world cruising, it looked and felt landlubberly.

The private railroad car flourished for about seventy years in America: in many ways it was grander, because more personalized, than hiring a whole train, which was not uncommon in Europe as well as the United States. Cars began in the 1870s, and did not completely disappear until Pearl Harbor. They had pretty names like 'Isabella' and 'Marchena', and cost about $25,000 in the 1880s, when Lily Langtry was given one called 'Lalee' by a playboy named Freddy Gebhard, as a mobile version of the apartment he had rented for her on West 53rd Street. By the First World War the price had trebled. They really were a home from home for the rich, with gold plate and servants who arrived at the touch of a mother-of-pearl bellpush. Some people, of course, really needed them, such as Jay Gould, who suffered from ulcers and had to drink a lot of milk provided by his own pedigree cow, who, like his doctor, always travelled with him. A certain Charlie Clark, son of a senator, had a car specially fitted with a sliding partition between his bedroom and the next, so that (at the touch of another pearl button) he could enjoy the company of whoever was adjacent. And Adolph Lewisohn, in his famous Depression spending spree, sometimes needed several railroad cars to transport his large staff who included secretary, stenographer, valet, chef, singing and dancing and French teachers, his private barber Purmann (who earned $3600 a year plus tips of up to $500 a time), and some of his Impressionist paintings that he might want to look at on the way.

And if you didn't actually want to own a private railroad car, you could always rent one, or several; like Anna Gould's brother George, who, wishing to take a party of friends to a winter sports festival in Canada, rented five Pullman cars at $500 a day each: a 'club car' which included a 'Moorish barber's shop', a dining car full of wood carved like a rood-screen, an 'observation sleeping car' with bathroom, an

36

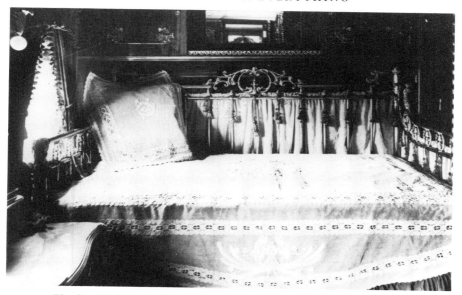

Charles M. Schwab the steel magnate's private railroad car *Loretto* (built by Pullman in 1901) boasted a king-sized bed in a mahogany-panelled state room. In 1913 he ordered an even bigger car of the same name.

ordinary sleeping car, and a 'parlor car' all in velvet; plus butlers, footmen and maids in livery. The guests wore evening dress most of the time.

The wearing of jewellery upon the person gives satisfaction to both the wearer and the beholder. It should be remembered that diamonds are *heavy*: it is quite an effort to carry them around. Mr Potter Palmer, the Chicago hotel and store owner, bought his wife, for many years the city's leading hostess, so many diamonds that she could scarcely stand upright. 'There she stands,' he would say fondly to his friends, 'with half a million on her back.' As a child, Evalyn Walsh, daughter of Tom Walsh of Washington, had been allowed to play with Mrs Palmer's jewels. This gave her an insatiable passion for jewels, so that even in the Depression, when she was not so rich any more, she could console herself by buying more and more of them – 'there's nothing like spending money as a cure for not having it', she observed cheerfully. By a chain of circumstances which we shall describe in the next chapter, she became the owner of two of the biggest diamonds in the world, the Star of the East and the Hope Diamond.

Not only women love diamonds. Ned Green – it comes as no surprise to note that he lived much of his life in Texas – loved diamonds almost as much as he loved girls, and even owned a diamond-studded chamberpot. Long before his time, in the 1860s, one of the main reasons for going to the opera in New York had been to look through opera glasses at other patrons to see what they were wearing. A certain Congressman John Morrissey, who ran gambling joints, had a special pair of opera glasses made in Paris for his wife. It was in the form of a lyre, all set in diamonds and sapphires, so that anyone looking at her through an ordinary pair of binoculars was liable to be blinded. It cost him $75,000.

The wearing of jewellery by men, we shall see, reached its ultimate possibilities in the state of Texas; and there were occasional outbreaks of it even among the New York Irish: thus J. F. McDonnell the financier, in the 1930s, was to be seen playing golf in diamond earrings and many bracelets that jingled as he addressed the ball.

There is, in fact, little point in owning diamonds if you don't show them to people. 'Them as has 'em, wears 'em,' was the belief of James Buchanan Brady, who had made much of his money from selling equipment to the railroad companies; and, he might have added with due modesty, *gives* 'em away. A teetotaller, he could never be sure that his dinner guests had had enough champagne until the wine waiter showed him a basket containing all the corks. Back in the Nineties Diamond Jim gave his guests diamond-studded watches and brooches worth up to $1000 each; and when the bicycling craze hit New York, gave all his friends gold-plated bicycles. He had jewellery designed in the form of vehicles, the stones always set in platinum – automobiles, coaches, locomotives and Pullman car shirt studs; and when the first aeroplanes appeared, he had lapel buttons designed in their image. It was thus possible for the wearer of all these things to carry an entire 'transportation set' on him. The whole collection was said to contain 2637 diamonds and twenty-one rubies, and was valued at over $87,000. He believed that you could add diamonds to everything. Bicycles should be not only gold-plated, they should be encrusted all over with jewels. Certain bicycle manufacturers refused to cooperate, thinking it would lower the tone of their machines, which would be ridden by the wrong class of person; and top jewellers such as Tiffany were inclined to agree. However, Diamond Jim did manage to get one or two diamond-and-gold bikes made, one of them costing $10,000, for the actress Lillian Russell. He told the cooperating jeweller: 'Mount some diamonds on the handlebars for class.'

4

GETTING ON IN SOCIETY

The *New York Sun* of 27 March 1883 described, in a series of gasps, an astonishing event at the 5th Avenue palace of Mr and Mrs William K. Vanderbilt. It was said to have cost $250,000, more than had ever been spent in America on one party. It was compared to the feast of Alexander the Great at Babylon, to the shows put on by Cleopatra for Mark Antony, and – inevitably – to the spectacular entertainments of Louis XIV (you could always please a New York hostess by mentioning the Sun King in the same breath). Alva Vanderbilt had not only excelled herself, she had outdone Alice Vanderbilt (Mrs Cornelius Vanderbilt II). Alice gave only silver gifts at her dances; Alva gave gold.

'Mrs W. K. Vanderbilt's Ball was gorgeously accomplished, with no interruption by dynamite,' the *Sun* reported; not ironically, for the odd anarchist, expressing his disapproval of high society with high explosive, was not unknown. The paper went on to describe 'a scene from Faeryland, Mother Goose, the Picture Galleries, the Courts and Camps of Europe, Audubon's Birds of America, Heathen Myths and Christian Legends', for such was the variety of fancy dress tableaux, which all took place amid 'a garden of flowers under bright lights to soft music from hidden instruments'. Baskets and urns full of hothouse roses, and palm trees hung with chains of orchids, had been arranged by Charles Klunder the florist. No doubt, the *Sun* said indulgently, Mrs Vanderbilt had been inspired by 'Mr Diedrich Knickerbocker's invaluable notes

39

Alice Vanderbilt makes history at her own fancy-dress ball – as an electric light.

Alice's arch-rival in society, Alva Vanderbilt, poses with artificial doves for a fashionable photographer.

on the fashions of New York a long time ago'. It was noted that Mr Jay Gould's name was not on the list of guests (he had swindled the Commodore long ago, and besides Alva considered him *nouveau riche* and common). The *New York World*, more prosaically, attempted a breakdown of the cost: costumes $155,730, flowers $11,000, carriage hire $4000, hairdressing $4000, and the rest was presumably accounted for by food, champagne, music and sundries. Another paper put the cost at only $75,000.

Alva was dressed as a Venetian princess; her sister Mrs Yznaga (who had married a rich Cuban) and Lady Mandeville (born Consuelo Yznaga) were Van Dyck portraits; William K. was the Duc de Guise, and his sisters were variously a marquise, a hornet and Little Bo-Peep; and Cornelius, clutching a diamond-encrusted sword, was Louis XVI. Only ex-President General Ulysses S. Grant wore ordinary evening dress, which for him *was* fancy dress. The dancing was interspersed with well-rehearsed Quadrilles, performed as 'square' or 'formation' dances. One of them was a Hobby-Horse Quadrille, for which the women wore red coats and white satin skirts, and the men red coats with white breeches: they were required to carry on their heads models of horses made of real horsehide.

The dramatic climax was the entry, rather late, of Mrs Caroline Astor – *the* Mrs Astor, whose visiting cards said simply 'Mrs Astor'. She too was dressed as a Venetian princess, and she outshone Alva Vanderbilt by wearing *all* her jewels. Yet the evening represented a decisive victory for Alva. The Astors had been leading Society for twenty years: they had gone up a class because they had moved their money out of trade into property. Transportation, in which the Vanderbilts had made most of their money, was still only trade. The Vanderbilts, for all their wealth, did not 'know' the Astors, nor could they buy boxes for the opera in the Golden Circle of the Academy of Music, not even for $30,000 of ready money. (This had so annoyed William Henry Vanderbilt that he had even conspired with his hereditary enemy Jay Gould to found the Metropolitan Opera in 1880.) Alva had been an aristocrat in her native Alabama: born Alva Smith, she was an impecunious Southern belle whose mother had brought her to New York after the Civil War to make a good marriage. This she had done, but it did not justify her being invited to Astor parties.

Many of Mrs Astor's parties had been organized by Ward McAllister, compiler of the famous '400' list of who was *in* Society. If there was a definition of the word 'debutante', it was probably 'a girl invited to

Mrs Astor's'. McAllister also was from the South. By inviting the Vanderbilts to his own parties, he had 'accepted' them. Now Alva tempted
him away from the Astors. Hearing that Alva Vanderbilt was giving
a ball of unprecedented splendour, Mrs Astor was worried. Her
daughter Carrie belonged to a dancing team called The Star Quadrille,
which expected to give an exhibition of dancing at all major social functions. But no Astors had been invited to 660 5th Avenue. So Mrs Astor
sank her pride and called on Alva, practically asking for an invitation.
She got it. The dancing, Quadrilles and all, went on until 4 a.m.; and
next winter season the Vanderbilts were invited to Mrs Astor's ball.

Alva had always made it clear that she considered it her *duty* to lead
Society. It was certainly hard work, and she had to be one jump ahead
of all rivals in ideas. Thus, in August 1889, she suddenly abandoned
orchids and hothouse roses and gave a ball in – of all places – the *stables*
of her 'cottage' at Newport, decorating them, like Harvest Festival,
with red peppers, pumpkins, turnips and eggplants. Society now
amused itself by trying to guess how *little* it had cost her.

To do her justice, Mrs Astor's vulgarity was not total. She seldom,
as one or two hostesses did, wrapped cigars and bread rolls in $100 bills
with her initials on them in gilt; and occasionally she did unheard-of
things such as inviting meritorious Jews. What she did perhaps overdo
(like Mrs Potter Palmer) was the wearing of jewellery. She had three
main styles of dress: white satin embroidered with pearls and silver with
a green velvet train; black satin with roses; and royal purple velvet
with gold paillettes. She had one diamond necklace of forty-four large
stones valued at $60,000, and another of 282 smaller stones, arranged
like the sun's rays, worth $80,000. Occasionally she sported Marie
Antoinette's stomacher. Even if you saw her from the rear, you could
not mistake Mrs Astor, for she had jewellery all down her spine too.
That was why she always sat bolt upright, because it was so painful
to lean against anything.

Caroline Astor's great annual ball was always held on a Monday in
January, in the famous 'art gallery ballroom' at 350 5th Avenue, amid
masses of flowers and mid-nineteenth-century French paintings. So far,
the Vanderbilts might have noted when they accepted their first invitation there, it was less impressive than their own home. But they had
not bargained for Mrs Astor's throne, a divan on a dais covered with
red silk. Here she sat, and if you were invited to sit beside her, it was a
Royal audience; many women who were not went home early in tears.
At half past one in the morning the Cotillion began, with John Lander's

orchestra playing; and dancers would be rewarded, the women with small pieces of jewellery, the men with buttonholes. Caroline's husband William was seldom present: he had usually run away to Florida to be on one of his two yachts. 'The sea air is so good for him,' Caroline would explain with a straight face. 'I would love to join him, but I'm such a bad sailor.'

The Vanderbilt men, too, were always less keen than their wives on this sort of thing, and sometimes ran away to hide on their yachts; but William K. did occasionally throw a party, preferably at Newport, and there is a record of one at which 'the masterpiece was a large owl on a perch, the bird being composed of 700 pieces of sugar and almonds. The eyes alone contained 60 pieces. A chain of confections in imitation of silver held the bird to his candied perch.'

From 1896 onwards, when she married Cornelius Vanderbilt III, and for the next fifty years, Grace Wilson reigned as 'the' Mrs Vanderbilt.

At Alva Vanderbilt's famous $250,000 fancy dress ball in 1883 – Mrs Frederick Rhinelander Jones, Miss Strong, Mrs Sandy, Mrs Francis Barlow, and a bear.

It was reckoned that she spent up to $300,000 a year on entertainments, which ranged from Sunday afternoon tea parties for sixty people at 'Vanderbilt Palace' on 5th Avenue to spectacular hospitality of Ziegfeld dimensions, at either 5th Avenue or Beaulieu Cottage at Newport, where she gave a *Fête des Roses* and an Oriental Ball, and parties at which the entire casts of Broadway shows were hired to entertain her guests, who included the Kings of Belgium, Spain and Siam, several Presidents, and Winston Churchill. Her husband, whose chief luxury was his yacht, which cost him $7000 a month to maintain, was not always present.

Alva had lost her title as 'the' Mrs Vanderbilt when in 1895 she was divorced. She became Mrs O. H. P. Belmont, wife of one of William K.'s friends who had frequently been a guest on the stormy voyages of the good ship *Alva*. Alice, Mrs Cornelius II, Grace's mother-in-law, was no longer a serious competitor. Besides, the game had changed; now it was a question of conquering *the* Mrs Astor. It was said that when *the* Mrs Astor died in 1908, the Society of Old New York died too. Thanks partly to Alva Vanderbilt's victory in 1883, there could never again be one single hostess who could keep outsiders out, or whom the *whole* of Society would follow like automata. When *the* Mrs Astor, in No. 7 box at the Metropolitan Opera (which was after all only a place 'to go on to after dinner') grew bored and left after the intermission, everyone else went too, and the cast sang to an empty house.

Grace Vanderbilt had one priceless advantage which the Astors lacked: she knew Royalty. She had once been engaged to Cecil Baring, son of Lord Revelstoke, and had met the Prince of Wales, afterwards Edward VII. She had also visited Potsdam and met the Kaiser. Her sister-in-law Gladys was married to a Hungarian Count. When, therefore, the Kaiser's brother, Prince Henry of Prussia, went to New York in February 1902, he accepted Grace's invitation to dinner. For him, as for all future Royal guests, Grace had a red carpet laid across the side-walk up the steps of her house and into the vestibule; and if it rained, and the carpet became muddy, it was simpler to buy a new one than to have the old one cleaned. Queens, Alva could not help noticing, dressed more simply than she did: thus Elisabeth, wife of King Albert of the Belgians, wore only one row of pearls.

Yet Mrs Astor had one triumph before she died: her last party, for only seventy-nine people, was a banquet in honour of Prince Louis of Battenberg: Royalty at last! And the Vanderbilts were not invited. As for Grace Vanderbilt, she survived two World Wars, spending and spending. She had moved into 640 5th Avenue, where her footmen wore dark red livery; and when the Second World War came, she moved out of 640 into 1048 5th Avenue, which had only twenty-eight rooms, where she could make do on $250,000 a year housekeeping money; and the great malachite urn' was given to the Metropolitan Museum of Art.

There was another social level of spending which attracted scandal, and which was never spoken of in the presence of *the* Mrs Astor or *the* Mrs Vanderbilt. There was the notorious New Year party given by his parents-in-law at which James Gordon Bennett, a pioneer of 'gee-whiz journalism', relieved himself publicly in the fireplace, a not very usual thing in New York at that time, and was challenged to a duel by his brother-in-law. Harry Lehr, a champagne salesman who unsuccessfully tried to replace Ward McAllister after his death in 1895, indulged in this kind of spending. Lehr, who had married a Miss Drexel Dahlgreen for her money, liked to be known as 'Society's court jester'. He gave a party with an elephant as guest of honour. Taken up by Mrs Stuyvesant Fish, he gave a similar dinner for a monkey at her Newport villa. He gave a banquet for 100 dogs (the menu: liver and rice, fricassee of bones and pâté de foie gras). He gave a fancy dress party where all the men had to dress as cats and give the ladies white mice as a surprise.

During the financial slump of 1896–7, there was a temporary feeling that lavish entertainment was out of place. So that what has come down to history as the Awful Seeley Dinner, at which a dancer called Little Egypt performed a belly dance on the table naked but for black silk stockings, all organized by Herbert Seeley, grandson of P. T. Barnum, made many people feel that the Astors and Vanderbilts were at least keeping up standards. Seeking to help the recession, Mrs Cornelius Sherman Martin in 1897 gave a ball for 900 people 'to stimulate trade'. The 'Bradley-Martin Ball' involved 6000 mauve orchids, several orchestras, and 400 carriages to take guests home afterwards. Everyone had to be in fancy dress representing an historical character. Mrs Bradley-Martin wore $100,000 worth of jewels, but was easily outdone by Mrs Astor's $200,000 worth. Long before it happened, the Ball was attacked by clergymen, and there was every expectation that it would be bombed by anarchists. However, there was a body of opinion which held that it would give employment to the needy, especially seamstresses and hairdressers, who were hired for the female guests at $15

To brighten up the 1897 slump, the famous Bradley-Martin Ball
(but no anarchists).

an hour. How much did it all cost? Well, the ballroom and supper
cost $4550, the fee for Victor Herbert's band was $658; otherwise we
have only various spectators' estimates, which vary between $100,000
and $370,000. The words 'bad form' were whispered. Worse, the dis-
play of wealth attracted the attention of the tax authorities. One way
or another, the Bradley-Martins found it prudent to leave America for
Scotland. And Oscar Hammerstein I wrote a burlesque about them
called *The Bradley-Radley Ball*.

The idea that spending creates employment, is almost a way of sharing wealth, rationalized the conduct of Marquis Boni de Castellane as

46

he spent his wife Anna's portion of the Gould millions. To celebrate her twenty-first birthday on 2 July 1897, in Paris, he conceived the idea of creating an illuminated ballet in the Bois de Boulogne. The three thousand guests (among them Marcel Proust, who took Boni as one of the models for Saint-Loup) trod on an estimated $9\frac{1}{2}$ miles of red carpet laid under the trees, lighted by 80,000 glass lamps specially made in Venice. Some 250 of the guests were invited to dinner in a marquee amid the overpowering scent of 25,000 roses. An orchestra of 200, the corps de ballet of the Opéra, and a huge display of fireworks, helped to attain an estimated cost of $250,000. Delighted to be back in his own country, Boni built a vast house, the Palais Rose at 45 Avenue du Bois, inevitably modelled on the Petit Trianon, with a red marble staircase ('bigger than the one at the Opéra!' said Anna), two ballrooms, and a theatre with 600 seats where he hoped to realize his dream of a private grand opera house. He also acquired one or two châteaux in the country. All set, you would think, for a full and happy life; but it was all too much for Anna, who in 1908 left him for another French aristocrat, Boni's cousin the Prince de Sagan, who was nineteen years older than Boni.

The weddings of the very rich are less competitive than one might expect, and one searches hard for examples of originality or offbeat lavishness. In 1895, with divorce hanging over her, Alva Vanderbilt gave a ball for 500 people at her Marble House at Newport, theoretically for her daughter Consuelo's coming-out. Consuelo was nineteen, a fairly advanced age for coming out, and her mother had just, by main force, prevented her from eloping with a playboy named Winthrop Rutherford. Alva had her eye on the young 9th Duke of Marlborough, twenty-four, who was made guest of honour. Whether he responded to the artificial garden which had been created complete with flowers, pools, fountains and stuffed humming birds, on the first floor, all lit up by hundreds of white silk Chinese lanterns, or to the music of two orchestras, we do not know. The Vanderbilts wanted a duke in the family, and Blenheim Palace was sorely in need of repairs and redecoration. The Duke was reasonably fond of the girl, and she, it was clearly understood, was not in love with him. He had courted her in New York during the great bicycle craze, and had been arrested for 'scorching' and (strictly forbidden) 'coasting' in Central Park with his feet on the handlebars of his penny-farthing. They were married at St Thomas Episcopal Church, to the music of a sixty-piece orchestra conducted by Walter Damrosch. Consuelo's dowry was £2 million, which, invested at three per cent, would yield an income of £60,000 a year; and the Duke's marriage settlement was the life interest on £2½ million of Vanderbilt railroad stock. The honeymoon was spent at 'Idle Hour', Alva's country mansion at Oakdale, Long Island.

Not until July 1940 were there nuptials which attracted the label 'wedding of the century', when Henry Ford II married Anne McDonnell of the Irish financial family. There was some discussion about whether to hold it in St Patrick's Cathedral, for Henry Ford II, by birth an Episcopalian, was taking instruction from Mgr Fulton Sheen; but the families finally decided on a church at Southampton which held only 500 people out of the 1100 invited.

The most wastefully yet cheerfully disastrous wedding of the century was a wholly Irish affair. At the wedding reception in June 1916 of Joseph Murray, son of millionaire Thomas E. Murray, and Mary Theresa Farrell, daughter of 'steel king' James A. Farrell, the house caught fire, $30,000 worth of wedding presents and $100,000 of furniture went up in smoke and rivulets of melting gold and silver, while the bride's father, with exemplary sang-froid, ran from room to room shouting: 'Don't worry – it's all insured!'

For the honeymoon of the century, we must go back to 1908. At the age of twelve, Evalyn, daughter of the Tom Walsh who had a throne room in his Washington house, had gone to school in her own blue carriage and pair driven by a Negro coachman in livery; so there was no question of her not being accustomed to luxury. That she should contemplate marriage at all with anyone known to her parents was a relief, since she had studied singing in Paris without success, given away a good deal of money to artists of no perceptible talent, and used the threat of marriage to an impoverished Italian prince as blackmail to make her father buy her a red Mercedes car. The Walshes were an accident-prone family, and it was not long before she escaped death in that Mercedes, in an accident near Newport which claimed the life of her brother Vinson.

When, therefore, she became engaged to Ned McLean, son of the man who published the *Washington Post*, it looked as if she might settle down to some kind of domesticity. She had an income of nearly $2 million a year, while Ned rubbed along on a measly $900,000. Papa Walsh and Papa McLean agreed, or perhaps hoped, that a honeymoon came only once in a lifetime, and that they would stump up $100,000 each 'for the young people to enjoy themselves'. They toured Europe, accompanied by a Miss Maggie Buggy, who had been Evalyn's nanny, spending and spending. In Leipzig, for some reason, Evalyn decided that a girl on her honeymoon needed more than one Mercedes, so they dashed back to Paris to buy another. Then, having done most of Europe, they went to Constantinople, where they had an introduction to the Sultan Abdul-Hamid, 'Abdul the Damned', who, with his empire breaking up all round him, cannot have been very pleased to see them. For Evalyn, who was crazy about diamonds, the high spot of the Constantinople trip was her visit to the Sultan's harem, where she instantly noticed, coveted, and never forgot, an outsize blue diamond round the neck of Abdul's leading lady.

On to Palestine, where Ned gave offence to people by wearing a fez with a white band around it, a privilege reserved for devout Muslims who had made a pilgrimage to Mecca. Hell, said Ned, he was entitled to wear it – he'd been to Mecca, and by Mecca he meant the

Mrs Edward B. McLean sporting the famous Hope Diamond.

Mecca Saloon in Cincinnati, where he had indulged his love of knocking men's hats off and buying them new ones, a hobby he may have learnt from James Gordon Bennett Jr, the newspaper proprietor, who adored pulling cloths off restaurant tables, scrupulously paying for the damage afterwards. There was by now not much of the $200,000 left, so they rushed back to Paris to have a last spending spree there. It took the form of a visit to Cartier's. If Evalyn could not have the blue diamond in Abdul's harem, she could at least have the Star of the East for 600,000 francs or $120,000. She and Ned hurried back to the States, leaving a trail of unpaid bills from Jerusalem to Cherbourg, and smuggled the diamond through the customs.

Next year their son Vinson was born, already famous as the '$100 million baby', and Evalyn's father died, leaving her richer than ever. It was clearly time for another spending honeymoon in Europe. Again, the centre of activity was Paris. At Cartier's Evalyn saw an enormous blue diamond – the very one she had seen on No. 1 Girl in Abdul the Damned's harem. She was told that this was the famous $44\frac{1}{2}$-carat Hope Diamond; that the previous owner had been a certain Habib Bey; that it had left the neck of No. 1 Girl when, in a palace revolution, she had been stabbed to death. Well, yes, the Hope Diamond, believed to have once belonged to Marie-Antoinette, did have a certain reputation for bringing ill-luck ... Evalyn bought it for $154,000, and, taking no chances, had a priest bless it. Back in Washington, she gave a $40,000 dinner party for forty-eight of her friends to show it to them.

Her spending was now partly transferred to little Vinson and his sister Evalyn. When they had a Christmas party it cost $15,000, and every child went away with an expensive toy, electric trains for the boys, and dolls as big as themselves for the girls. When Ringling Brothers' circus was in town, they did not go to it, it came to them, for an exclusive command performance. The children rode in a miniature coach with three tiny horses that had once belonged to the midget General Tom Thumb. In the winter they wore ermine suits made for them by Worth in Paris. It might have been the Hope Diamond that brought them a share of misfortune; or it might have been the Macleans whose misfortune brought them to the Hope Diamond. Most of the bad luck went to Ned, who became an alcoholic and gave a bottle of whisky a day to his equally unlucky pet seal. But Evalyn did very nearly achieve her life's ambition, which was 'to die bankrupt'. When she died, she left a little over $606,000, which by her standards was poverty.

5

ORIENTAL SPLENDOUR

---

*W*hatever the faults of the Indian Princes, they did lend colour to the British Raj. Evalyn Walsh McLean had nothing on the Gaekwar of Baroda, whose court dress was of spun gold fabric woven by a single family, who grew their finger nails very long so that they could use them as teasing combs. Among his thousands of diamonds was the seventh largest in the world, the Star of the South, from Brazil. The Maharaja of Patiala, whose pearl necklace was insured at Lloyd's for $1 million, had a breastplate composed entirely of diamonds, said to number 1001. Like many Indian princes, one of the Maharajas of Gwalior revered Queen Victoria so much that he wanted an even bigger chandelier in his palace than the biggest in Buckingham Palace, and every piece of glass in it was specially made in Venice. But would the roof of his palace stand its weight? He resolved the matter by having his largest elephant lowered on to the roof by a crane to test its strength: the roof did not collapse.

The Maharaja of Mysore's palace, with 600 rooms, many of them filled with stuffed beasts he and his family had hunted and killed, was bigger than that of any European monarch. The familiar Versailles fantasy struck the Maharaja of Kapurtala, who actually believed himself to be a reincarnation of Louis XIV. He hired French architects, designers and experts on French *objets d'art* to build a replica of Versailles in the foothills of the Himalayas, and fill it with everything that was to be found at the Sun King's court, even forcing his Sikh servants to abandon their puggris for powdered wigs to go with the silk coats and breeches and buckled seventeenth-century shoes which became their uniform. Only the seventh Nizam of Hyderabad earned an undying reputation for meanness. His guests were always offered one cup of tea, one biscuit and one cigarette; and after they had gone, he smoked the stubs left in the ashtray. The most generous act of his life was to contribute £25 million to the British exchequer for the prosecution of the First World War.

The Raj had been preceded by the East India Company, which no longer had a monopoly of trade. As the British flourished in India, Bombay became a boom city; and in noisy, fetid Tamarind Lane lived the Sassoon family. They were not the first Bagdad Jews in Bombay – the Nissims, Gabbais, Shamoons and Settys were already there, and so was the merchant princedom of Jardine, Matheson & Forbes. The Sassoons built up their capital by lending money and claiming repayment with interest in goods, not money. They kept themselves to themselves, employing no local labour: their staff were all Jews from Bagdad. David Sassoon, who had led the exodus from Bagdad by way of Persia, laid down the principle of owning warehouses, not ships. The Sassoons were as secret as the Astors were ostentatious. Never as rich as the Vanderbilts or the Rothschilds, they were more worldwide; indeed they split into two hostile branches, both ultimately destined to take root in Britain, but still so divided that one branch went to Eton, the other to Harrow.

The division began in 1844 when David sent his son Elias to China to open up a trade in opium and textiles, especially cotton. The most likely ports were Shanghai and Hong Kong, where, again, Jardine, Matheson were already established (the Sassoons seldom if ever pioneered), and of these Shanghai seemed to offer the better opportunities. Here, in an organization that was to become the Hong Kong and Shanghai Banking Corporation, the Sassoons traded in innumerable commodities. It was understood that a substantial fund would have to be set aside for the bribery of customs officials. Elias indeed went beyond his instructions and entered the East Indies spice trade as well, and when August Belmont's father-in-law, Commodore Perry, concluded a commercial treaty with Japan, Elias was not far behind.

The Bombay Sassoons were now prosperous enough to move out of the city to cool and peaceful bungalows on Malabar Hill and as far away as Poona. Before his death in 1864, old David built his dream house in Palladian style, on Malabar Hill, and called it Sans Souci.

David Sassoon, merchant prince and philanthropist, founder of a dynasty.

Meanwhile Elias's brother Abdullah, who changed his name to Albert, had been sent to London to join another brother Sassoon D. Sassoon ('S.D.'). In no time, it seemed, Albert was a millionaire (or rather, he lived, more obviously than his brothers, the life of a millionaire). A family so stretched across the world must surely split, and the occasion was the rivalry between Albert and Elias. Elias settled the matter for some years by breaking away from the rest of the family and founding his own company, E. D. Sassoon & Son, in competition with his brothers. Albert had been made a baronet, because, like many Sassoons, he spoke Persian (the Sassoons had been founders of the Imperial Bank of Persia), and had thus been able to entertain the Shah during his visit to England in 1889 and so help to secure a sixty-year concession to exploit the mineral wealth of Persia. Albert was now English of the English, with two great houses, 25 Kensington Gore, and 1 Eastern Terrace, Kemp Town, Brighton. There was little of the oriental in his town house, with its Jacobean dining room and fireplace over which hung an enormous tapestry depicting his adored Queen Victoria; with the addition of ebony and carved ivory which he had picked up from the

Prince of Wales's Pavilion at the 1878 Paris Exposition. And, striving to be a part of Olde England, he had six tapestries representing scenes from *The Merry Wives of Windsor.*

The Sassoon women, almost in purdah while they remained in India, flowered in London. The Sassoons were joining a new business aristocracy that gathered round the Prince of Wales at Marlborough House – Sir Ernest Cassel, Baron de Hirsch, various Rothschilds, men like Barney Barnato, who had made sudden millions in South African gold and diamonds, Sir Thomas Lipton. The sons of 'S.D.' had wives who rivalled each other as hostesses, and united only in efforts to outdo the Rothschild wives. Thus Louise, who came from the Russian banking family of de Gunzbourg to marry 'S.D.'s' son Joseph, gave a ball at her house in Albert Gate for which she hired Johann Strauss's orchestra yet, with extraordinary restraint, offered only hot and cold soups instead of the usual buffet supper. Mrs Arthur Sassoon, however, had no such inhibitions; nor had her French chef. Neither had much respect for anyone's liver. One of her famous menus began with quails stuffed with pâté, followed by terrines of turtle, ortolans from France artificially fattened, Scotch salmon, and the speciality of the house, 'coffee-cake soaked in cognac and served flambé with ice-cream and hot stewed cherries'. This last was a gesture of defiance to Mrs Louise Rothschild, whose liqueur-soaked chocolate gâteau was so celebrated. When, in the fullness of time, a Sassoon (Albert's son Edward) married a Rothschild (Alice), the rivalry subsided a little.

Sassoon boys now went to English public schools (it was the E. D. Sassoon side of the family that preferred Harrow to Eton). The family business still stretched from India to China and beyond, and most of them were in it. Some had dual nationality, such as Philip, born in 1888, who was both British and French. With Philip and Victor Sassoon, the family reached its summit of magnificence. Both were 'third Baronets', Philip as the grandson of Albert and Victor as the grandson of Elias. Both embraced, rather late, the dandyism of the 1890s, w's for r's, Bertie Wooster monocles and all. In Philip's case it was observed by Osbert Sitwell, who was his fag at Eton, and whom Philip, breaking the usual rules of such a relationship, invited home for the holidays.

Philip was more obviously rich than his cousin Victor. Was it a pose when, missing a train, he said to the stationmaster 'Bwing me another'? At Oxford he was out of fashion: there, just before 1914, the aesthete-athlete was king, and by one of them, Julian Grenfell, he was chased with a whip. The cousins had, on and off, three main houses. At 45

Park Lane, Philip kept his pictures, his eighteenth-century furniture, his tapestries and Aubusson carpets. Only in the ballroom, with its mirrors and glass walls, where a ball for four hundred guests could be given, did the visitor feel himself suddenly transported to the East.

Philip played polo with the Prince of Wales and Winston Churchill at Roehampton, but it was Victor who was more obviously physical. As soon as Blériot had flown the Channel, Victor yearned to fly, and became a founder-member of the Royal Aero Club. It followed that, wishing to buy a country manor, he should choose Port Lympne, next to an airfield, overlooking Romney Marsh, with a distant view on a clear day of Cap Gris Nez. At Port Lympne, described by Chips Channon in his diary as 'a triumph of beautiful bad taste and Babylonian luxury, with terraces and flowery gardens and jade-green pools and swimming baths and rooms done up in silver and blue and orange', there were more than a hundred rooms and accommodation for forty guests at a time. Sometimes the guests were a political event, as in 1920, when Lloyd George, President Millerand and their staffs met in the Anglo-French Conference to discuss German reparations after the war. At other times the guests ranged from the Prince of Wales to Mrs Dudley Ward (which was not very far) and from Charlie Chaplin to T. E. Lawrence. The rooms were frequently redecorated to match what Philip considered to be the personality of the guest – thus Charlie Chaplin found himself sleeping in yellow and gold. Guests used Philip's private beach at Dymchurch for bathing. In the garden were 130 marble steps, a Moorish patio with fountains, a cloister of glazed tiles brought from Spain, and a collection of rare water-birds. The house had its own pumping station and its own bakery which provided four different kinds of warm bread for breakfast. And for almost every other meal, treacle pudding, the favourite dish of this prince of pleasure, was on the menu.

Philip's private aeroplane, a Super Moth with central heating, painted in the colours of the Old Etonian tie, was used like a taxi to fly to breakfast with friends in the next county, or over to Paris to see a new play. Trustee of the National Gallery, Conservative MP for Hythe from 1912 until his death in 1939, and Under-secretary of State for Air in two governments, Philip was hated by Socialists. It was perhaps Osbert Sitwell who said that 'his baroque was worse than his bite'.

His third house, Trent Park, took him many years to transform into what Osbert Sitwell called 'a kind of paradise' and Harold Nicolson found it so overdecorated that 'even his friends' had become 'mere pieces of decoration'. In the Park's thousand acres there was however plenty of room for such up-to-date amenities as a private airfield and a nine-hole golf course, where Philip had his own golf pro. Philip had taken a mid-Victorian mansion of mauve brick and rebuilt it in rose-red brick and stone, filling the gardens, Sitwell says, with 'statues and lead sphinxes, smiling from their pedestals, and shepherds fluting under ilex groves, and orangeries and fountains and pyramids...' Amid this splendour, Nicolson says, Philip's 'un-English little figure ... flitted among those vast apartments, removed from the ordinary passions, difficulties and necessities of life.' Here his hospitality was even more aesthetic. The drainpipes were painted gold. Normally he flew a Union Jack from a turret, but one evening he hauled it down 'because the colours clashed with the sunset'. He sent orchids to women guests as they dressed for dinner, and highly-scented carnations to the men (accompanied by a jug of ready-mixed dry Martini). Even the shrubs round the heated marble swimming pool were scented. In some rooms, the flowers were dyed to match the curtains. In the grounds, you were asked not to feed the king penguins, because Philip liked to do this himself.

Victor, an altogether more outgoing character who died in 1961 aged eighty, having married an American nurse when he was seventy-seven, was known as 'the J. P. Morgan of the Orient'. Living variously at the Cathay Hotel in Shanghai, where, in the 1930s, he was still giving bright-young-people-type fancy dress parties (at one of them he had clowns and performing animals, with himself as ringmaster, an idiosyncrasy he shared with Alfred Rothschild), on his houseboat and at his bungalow in Hungjao Road, he seemed always to be surrounded by Chinese servants. As in the West Philip had grown more and more oriental, so in the East Victor became more and more western: his bungalow, 'Eve's', was a replica of a Tudor-Jacobean house with exposed timbers and open fireplaces and inglenooks. During the Second World War he lived at the Taj Mahal Hotel, Bombay, the city where his family's wealth had begun. He diversified the family business into property, insurance, development in the Bahamas, horses. 'There is only one race greater than the Jews,' he said, 'and that is the Derby.' In 1953 he won the Coronation Derby with Pinza, ridden by Gordon Richards. He shared with his cousin Philip a love of nursery food. If there was one frustration in his life, it was that his chef refused to make shepherd's pie – 'I'm a rich man, and I *never* get it!'

The Sassoons were merchant princes, but the Aga Khans were more.

56

A day at the races – the Aga Khan at Longchamps.

They too bring us back to British India, for it was the first of them who helped Sir Charles Napier to conquer Sind. The fourth and present one, Karim, is said to be 'more powerful than the Pope' because his duties to millions of Ismaili Muslims in three continents are both spiritual and temporal. His empire embraces investments, insurance, the Aga Khan Bank in Asia, jute mills, marble quarries, a chain of newspapers in East Africa, stables and stud farms in Ireland, Muslim schools, hospitals, playing fields and housing estates in Africa and Asia, interests in about seventy different industries in Switzerland, Pakistan and Africa; and, since 1969, a whole new tourist area in the north of Sardinia, with hotels, real estate, supermarkets, boats, an airline, shops and discothèques.

The Aga Khan is infallible. When asked why he, a Muslim, drank alcohol, which was forbidden to his subjects, Aga Khan III (grandfather of the present one) replied: 'I am so holy that when I touch wine it turns to water.' His bath water was bottled like wine and sold to the Faithful. Descended forty-seventh in direct line from the Prophet's daughter Fatima, Aga Khan III (1877–1957) left an even more vivid impression on Britain in the 1920s and 1930s than his extravagant, inexhaustible son Aly. It was his mother, Lady Ali Shah, who guided the family into sound investment, a tradition carried on by her great-grandson. For Aga Khan III, horses were both a hobby and a business, and one fact everybody in Britain knew about him was that he had 'won the Derby five times'; another was that he had been married several times. His first wedding, to his cousin Shahzadi, was shared with Shahzadi's brother Shamsruddin, who was also getting married. Bombay had seldom seen anything like it. Said to have cost £50,000, the double wedding went on for sixteen days, with music, sword dances, acrobats, and clowns, with never a drop of anything stronger than lime-juice. Ismaili imams, British Government, Army and Diplomatic representatives and Indian Princes who were among the guests must have expected that anything which took so long must have something permanent about it.

Aga Khan II is weighed in diamonds for his Diamond Jubilee in Bombay, 1946 – yielding £640,000 for Ismaili Moslems.

But Aga Khan III was restless. It was his duty and pleasure to escape to Europe, where he could meet European royalty and the society which was then so important to any ruler. He founded the Muslim League in India, and he built a palace, the Yarooda at Poona, for half a million rupees to give employment to some of his subjects. Then he went off on his travels – to the Riviera, to London, to Queen Victoria at Windsor, to New York; above all, to Monte Carlo, where he became passionately interested in opera and ballet. Especially ballet: in Monte Carlo he met the prima ballerina Teresa Magliano, who was nineteen, and married her in Cairo in 1908. Their first son died young; their second, born in 1911, was the unforgettable Aly Khan.

Aga Khan III now had a permanent suite at the Ritz in London, and was obsessed (yet shrewdly so) with horses, on which he had spent £100,000 in three years. He now had George Criticos ('George of the Ritz', who had risen far above his job as a hall porter) as his London agent. His chocolate and green colours were to be seen at all big race meetings in the twenty years between the World Wars. And he was disposed to marry again, which he did in 1929: his new bride was Jane-André Carron, a Roman Catholic, on whom he settled £200,000. They were married by the Mayor of Aix-les-Bains in December 1929.

In his sixtieth year, 1936, Aga Khan III weighed something over 220 pounds. This was significant, because it was also the year of his Golden Jubilee Durbar in Bombay, and his subjects proposed to weigh him in gold in gratitude for his fifty-year reign. He tipped the scales at 335,000 rupees, or £25,760. Another Golden Jubilee in East Africa yielded a similar weight of gold, which was spent on scholarships for young Ismailis.

When war came in 1939, Aga Khan III went to live in the Palace Hotel, St Moritz. Was it because he thought Britain was going to be defeated? The family denies it. Certainly he was short of money, being unable to transfer it to Switzerland. He sold two of his Derby winners, Mahmoud and Bairam, for £60,000, and afterwards claimed that his family lived on this money until 1946. Yet he was not too depressed to marry again, which he did in 1944. ('Our family,' he used to say when discussing either marriage or horses, 'has always had mating problems.') The new Begum, Yvette Labrousse, had been 'Miss France 1930': for her he built a new villa on the Riviera called 'Yakimour'.

Two years later came his Diamond Jubilee. From Ismailis all over the world, by battleship and flying boat, the diamonds poured into Bombay. He was now twelve pounds heavier than he had been at his

Prince Aly Khan, deputising for his father at the Aga Khan III's Platinum Jubilee in 1957, inspects the offerings – valued at Rs. 3 million.

Golden Jubilee, and his weight in diamonds yielded £640,000 in Bombay and £684,000 in Nairobi. The money was spent on schools and other philanthropic projects. There was just time, before he died in 1957, to organize a Platinum Jubilee, which realized three million rupees, with which an Ismaili finance and investment trust was set up.

He had loved women and horses and money, but not entirely to the detriment of his Imâmate. Therefore he disapproved of the son who might have succeeded him, Aly Khan. The delight of debutantes and the despair of their mothers (unless, as sometimes happened, they too were involved with him), this mad, romantic, lavish, irresponsible young man, operating from a small house in Mayfair, swept in an Alfa-Romeo through London society in the late 1920s and 1930s, dancing all night at the Embassy, the 400, the Café de Paris, always with a different girl. Girls boasted of having affairs with him: he had, it seems, a special technique for prolonging pleasure . . .

There was a time when it seemed that he was about to marry Thelma, Lady Furness, friend of the Prince of Wales. They met in New York; he followed her back to London and pursued her with daily mountains of roses, and for a whole London season was seen with no one else. This had a permanent effect on history in that, while Thelma was in New York, the Prince of Wales met Wallis Simpson and so was lost to her for ever. Eventually, in 1934, Aly met Mrs Loel Guinness, formerly Joan Yarde-Buller, and married her.

The marriage lasted thirteen years, somehow surviving the war. Aly's life was now partly centred on the Riviera, where he bought the Château de l'Horizon, between Nice and Cannes, for a mere £30,000. At Palm Beach Casino, Cannes, he met Rita Hayworth, who had been Mrs Orson Welles for the past four years and had by him a daughter, Rebecca. The wedding of Aly and Rita, on 27 May 1947, by the Mayor of Vallauris at his town hall, and the reception afterwards at the Château de l'Horizon, have passed into rich-rich history. The wedding dress came from Jacques Fath, whose top model, Bettina, would be Aly's last love. The best man was General Georges Catroux, late commander of Free French forces in Lebanon. The pool at the Château had been filled with thousands of litres of eau de Cologne (another version says that it was white wine) on which floated a huge chain of white carnations in the shape of the letter M (Rita being short for Margerita); and an orchestra, the strings of which were on the roof to give a ghostly effect, played Aly's two favourite songs, 'Smoke Gets in Your Eyes' and 'La Vie En Rose'. It was understood that Rita was to have a dress allowance of £4000 a year.

They were divorced six years later. Then there was an interlude with Gene Tierney, who had a nervous breakdown; and then, of course, there was Bettina. Now the Château de l'Horizon and Aly's Paris house in the Boulevard Maurice Barrès were often so full of guests, invited and uninvited, that their host could find no room for himself; not that he always remembered whom he had invited. Sometimes his guests were people who had rendered him a service of some kind: the switchboard operator at the Ritz always had her summer holiday at the Château.

His downfall was fast cars. Being always late for everything, and making other people late too, he invariably drove too fast. When the President of Pakistan visited Paris, and had to be driven to the airport, he and his wife, rigid with terror, found Aly himself at the wheel; leaving the police escort on their motorcycles far behind, they were hurtled to Orly at 80 mph. This happened once too often. Due to be at a dinner party at 8 pm on the night of 12 May 1960, he had not turned up by 10 pm. Hostesses were used to this: sometimes he forgot to come at all. Next to women and horses, he loved speed. He just had to try out his new Lancia car. Near St Cloud he pulled out to overtake a car, and crashed head-on into another coming in the opposite direction.

In one of his sons, Sadruddin, something of his spirit lived on. Sadruddin married Nina Dyer, another model who had been married to Heinrich von Thyssen, having settled half a million pounds on her and enriched her world with a Caribbean island, a panther, and a villa at Versailles where it was her fancy to keep 200 parrots. But his other son, Karim, was different. He was destined to succeed his grandfather as Aga Khan, and would have a worldwide empire to run. He enjoyed luxury, but he could take it or leave it. His further education took place at Harvard School of Engineering, where he registered as 'K. Khan'. He had no car, wore jeans, and was known to his room-mate, Adlai Stevenson's son John, as 'the guy with one pair of shoes'. This was the man who, prompted by his half-brother Patrick Guinness, would turn thirty-five miles of the Costa Smeralda, Sardinia, into a playground for celebrities who were spearheaded by Princess Margaret, various Rockefellers and Rothschilds, Danny Kaye, the Chaplins and both Bettina and Rita Hayworth.

6

SUPER-SPENDER

---

*W*hen I grow up, Momma, can I live in Windsor Castle? . . . Well then, will you buy me the Louvre?' Dear little chap: William Randolph Hearst, aged about ten, trying out his palace fantasies on his mother, who, many years later, would say in perplexity: 'Every time Willie feels badly, he goes out and buys something.' Accepting, for a moment, the *Citizen Kane* diagnosis of Hearst, we may wonder whether he would ever have bothered to build San Simeon if he had been a senator like his father, or if (since he would have bought this too) he had eventually been President of the United States. And we may still come up with the answer: yes, he would. He graduated to palaces by way of a large number of smaller, art-crammed dwellings.

Being an inheritor, he did not have to make his first eight million. It seemed to him that by spending, he automatically acquired fresh wealth. Things bought might be expected to appreciate in value, so that spending was investing. For a number of years, this boom-psychology worked. His newspapers, magazines and radio stations brought him profits of $400 million. He never really looked at the publications he bought to see if they were viable. In the 1890s he was reckoned to be spending $1 million a year on newspapers. (Yet he was a slow payer of bills, and took a delight in having 'doubles' impersonate him when leaving his office to escape ever-waiting creditors, some with summonses, outside the door.) His method of staffing a newspaper was to lure top writers away from other papers and pay them unheard of

salaries; and there were always ample funds for stunts, which were apt to involve 'special trains, balloons and grizzly bears'; and of course, in 1898, a war.

'Buying the Louvre' was not so fantastic to a boy who grew up, as Hearst did, in such houses as La Hacienda del Poco de la Verona, in California, which contained a wing called by his mother 'the Boys' House' with thirteen bedrooms for grandchildren, nurses, governesses, tutors. The whole ground floor was one huge playroom, with every toy, game, exercise gadget and novelty ever conceived by man for the entertainment of children. When he grew up, he did not at first do as Vanderbilts and Astors did – build huge Gothic or Renaissance houses on 5th Avenue or Rhode Island. He would buy a small place, fill it with curios and *objets d'art*, and when it became too full, move into a larger place. In his early New York days he occupied the whole third floor of the Worth Hotel on 25th Street, which he fashioned to his taste by building in oak beams (fake) and antique tiles (genuine), and cramming it with 'art'. He then bought a four-storey house on Lexington Avenue which had once belonged to President Chester Arthur, and soon there were so many German suits of armour, Egyptian mummy cases, and antlers and tusks of various large beasts over doors and fireplaces and sticking out of walls, and so many shelves of pottery, that the Hearst family could scarcely move without either smashing something frail of priceless value or impaling themselves. So he must move house again, this time to a block of flats. The top three floors with thirty rooms should be enough, he thought; but he bought the whole block so that he could knock down walls and build a baronial hall inside if he wanted to. And if he should happen to be in Los Angeles, a whole floor of the Ambassador Hotel awaited him. There were other apartments in other cities which one of Hearst's biographers coyly describes as 'undisclosed snuggeries'.

The palace fantasy began to take practical shape in 1917 when Hearst, a married man of fifty-four, went backstage at the New Amsterdam theatre, New York, where *Ziegfeld Follies of 1917* was playing, and met a Miss Douras, aged twenty, who used the name Marion Davies. For her he would build a castle where she should reign as Fairy Queen. Miss Davies, who had a slight stutter which made everything she said seem funnier than it was, should also become the greatest film-star in the world. Into both projects William Randolph Hearst would pour money until they became fact. Marion must become bigger than Mary Pickford, and Hearst must buy into Hollywood until he became the

Above San Simeon on the Enchanted Hill – the sight that made Cecil Beaton say 'Gosh!'.

Below The entrance of La Casa Grande – each stone shipped from a castle in Spain. Hearst's bedroom suite, with balcony, was directly above the front door.

biggest producer of the biggest, most expensive films. He would hire
the most expensive scenario writer of the day, Frances Marion, who
was paid $2000 a week. The sets would be designed by Joseph Urban,
who had designed the Ziegfeld Theatre and a number of super-cinemas.
Hearst saw Marion as an eternal virgin in historical romance. Not pos-
sessed of a great feeling for history (though he liked sleeping in Charles
I's bed), he was nevertheless fanatical about the accuracy of period
props, and to this end he used his own antiques lavishly to embellish
Urban's sets.

Few cinema buffs will remember *When Knighthood Was in Flower*,
and a revival of it today would be a riot. This epic of 1922 was matched
with music by Victor Herbert, veteran of many operettas and Ziegfeld
shows, whose 'Marion Davies March' publicized the star. A romance
set in the internecine strife of the Tudor era, it was billed as 'the greatest,
most costly and most beautiful photoplay ever produced, from the
sweetest story ever told'. There were four other epics, all made by
Hearst's Cosmopolitan Films within the MGM organization, and all
showing Marion ($10,000 a week), whose natural gifts were for
comedy, as purity in costumed distress: only *Lights of Old Broadway*,
however the balance sheets were presented, could be said to have spun
any money. Could she please play Sadie Thompson in *Rain*? Certainly
not. Well, then, Elizabeth Barrett in *The Barretts of Wimpole Street*?
This led to Hearst's break with MGM, for Irving Thalberg was in charge
of casting, and it was Norma Shearer (Mrs Thalberg) who got the part.
Cosmopolitan Films went over to Warner's; and here was an unfore-
seen difficulty. For Marion Davies had built herself a $75,000 'bunga-
low' with fourteen rooms, all filled with antiques, at Culver City on
the MGM lot. Would she now sell it and build another at Warners? She
would not. The bungalow was treated as an ancient monument and
transported, piece by piece, on rollers across Hollywood.

By now, part of the palace fantasy had been realized – part, because
Hearst was never a man to be content with one palace. From 1919
onwards a little middle-aged lady who still dressed in Edwardian hats
and skirts and wore very large glasses had been turning the childlike
medieval imaginings of Hearst into marble. Julia Morgan, an architect
who had studied at the Ecole des Beaux-Arts, had been a friend of his
mother's, and so presumably knew what she was in for. Miss Morgan's
task indeed was never finished, so many alterations were there to her
plans. From 1919 onwards into the 1930s, there were up to 150
workmen at San Simeon, either building something or pulling some-

'Pops' with Marion Davies towards the end of his life. Marion had
lent him $1 million when the Depression hit his publishing empire.

thing down in order to erect it somewhere else.

San Simeon, built in 48,000 acres of land which Hearst's father had
once bought for sixty cents an acre, when it was known as Piedra
Blanca, was always called 'the ranch' because Hearst's father had built
a holiday cabin there many years before. Later, with land additions,
it grew to about 600 square miles, 'half the size of Rhode Island' or
a little smaller than Hertfordshire. It put Hearst into the Louis XIV
class: Versailles was a back-yard by comparison. It was – a great satisfaction – bigger than George Vanderbilt's 'Biltmore' in North Carolina.
Hearst, abetted by Miss Morgan, chose a hill with only a few trees on

it, about 2000 feet high. It had been known, probably because of family picnics there many years before, as Camp Hill. Hearst rechristened it The Enchanted Hill, and, to suit the Spanish dream in his mind, translated it into La Cuesta Encantada. Four fantastic buildings were to rise upon it: La Casa Grande, for Marion and himself, and three guest houses, La Casa del Monte, La Casa del Sol and La Casa del Mar. They were to be reached by a six-mile driveway from the main road. Everything had to be as he imagined it. Approaching one of the buildings from the driveway, he thought it made an ill-balanced picture: so naturally it was demolished and rebuilt a few yards away. The two main towers of La Casa Grande also gave trouble: they looked at first too forbidding, so they were pulled down and redesigned with more ornamentation.

San Simeon had its own airfield, stud farms, dairies, cattle ranch (with 10,000 head of beef cattle), poultry farms and a zoo; and visitors usually arrived in Hearst's private train. Conservative guesses at what it cost to run all this have settled on $6000 a day. In one sense, La Casa Grande was never finished, for in two acres of cellars lay the famous unpacked *objets d'art*; and he might at any moment buy a Cistercian cloister somewhere in Europe and have it transported stone by stone to California, before figuring out how he could add it to San Simeon. Hearst and Marion lived in what was called the Celestial Suite, on the third floor, their apartments connected by a long sitting room inside the building and a covered balcony outside. The black carved wood bed in which Hearst slept had once belonged to Cardinal Richelieu. It went without saying that, in their black marble bathrooms, the taps were gold-plated. From the Celestial Suite they descended to the ground floor in a special richly carved elevator with an Old Master on each wall. This vehicle also took Hearst to his medieval Gothic study in one of the turrets.

Around San Simeon were landscaped gardens, with a permanent staff of two dozen gardeners led by an Englishman, Nigel Keep. Like Alfred Krupp, Hearst remade nature to suit his dream: rocks were dynamited to make valleys, cypresses were brought from thirty miles away and transplanted, pines were made to grow in soil not generally liked by conifers. In 1924 Hearst bought forty buffalo from Montana at $1000 each as the nucleus of what was intended to be the largest private zoo in America if not in the world. Soon he had more than a hundred different kinds of animal. Along the driveway were notices: 'Animals have the right of way,' and if one stood in the path of your car you waited – perhaps an hour – for it to go away.

Yet there were moments of magic at San Simeon. When there was mist on the Enchanted Hill, the floodlit towers of La Casa Grande appeared as if hanging in the sky. Cecil Beaton, a guest there for New Year's Eve 1930, could scarcely find words for his first sight of it. 'At the top of a tree-spotted mountain,' he told his diary, 'we caught sight of a vast, sparkling white castle in Spain. It was right out of a fairy story. "Gosh," I said.' There seemed to be footmen for each of about forty guests. 'My room seemed gigantic,' Beaton continued. 'There was a carved gilt ceiling; great hewn Jacobean beds with gold brocade covers; old, tinselled velvets hanging on the walls.' La Casa Grande 'loomed like Wells Cathedral, with an assembly room and a dining-room both the size of a great church'. Some of the statues, dotted here and there among the cypresses in the garden, were, he said, 'not up to scratch'; yet 'we'd been so overpowered by Donatellos and Della Robbias that it made the place come alive to see a nymph with bobbed hair eating an apple'.

Cecil Beaton had arrived with Anita Loos, Colleen Moore and others by the Hearst train from Los Angeles which arrived at San Luis Obispo at two o'clock in the morning. Guests, after an all-night party on board, were expected to sleep until breakfast; then a porter would go the length of the train shouting: 'It's after nine o'clock and Mr Hearst is up.' Ten of San Simeon's thirty-five limousines drove the guests forty miles to San Simeon. Guests, he found, were free to do anything, and indeed were left on their own most of the time. If you wandered through the Italian gardens, filled with fountains and classical statuary, you could at any time or place summon a servant to bring you a drink, for there were telephones concealed in rocks, in trees, and all round the swimming pool, and three switchboard operators were constantly at work. If you had brought the wrong clothes, you simply asked a maid or a valet to bring the right ones, supplied in your size by Hearst. Hearst and Marion might be there to receive you, or they might not, or only one of them might be there – the only difference it made was that if Marion were there without him, everyone Charlestoned and drank a lot and sometimes wrecked priceless pieces of furniture; and the sudden entry of a scowling Hearst could freeze the party into silence. At such times Marion soothed him, calling him Pops. Hearst's idea of a good time was either a picnic or a film show.

A picnic – for which you could borrow riding kit as well as a horse – was an elaborate trek of anything up to forty miles (you were still on the ranch at that distance) with field kitchens, barbecues, packmules, lanterns for when darkness fell, sleeping bags for an overnight camp, and occasionally a band. Never let it be said that Hearst did not have fun with his wealth. A film show meant, too often, sitting through one of Marion's old movies in San Simeon's 200-seat private cinema. This was the almost invariable programme after dinner if Hearst were there, and it was compulsory.

For dinner, guests gathered in the Assembly Hall waiting for Hearst and Marion to appear from the Celestial Suite, which was scheduled to happen at nine o'clock but sometimes happened much later, so that guests drank too many cocktails while waiting for food that was either cold or oven-dried. Observers have drawn attention to the ketchup bottles and paper napkins that always appeared on San Simeon dinner tables, attributing them to Hearst's bad taste or meanness. There is a simpler explanation: they reminded him (just as the picnics reminded him) of his boyhood on Piedra Blanca ranch before he transformed it into a Spanish castle. As for the food, he was anything but mean: among many stories is the one about his chartering an aeroplane to bring shrimps from Louisiana.

Marion Davies, always surrounded by an entourage of her own, mostly girls, was a millionairess in her own right, and a generous

William Randolph Hearst and friends at San Simeon in the late 1920s. Note ketchup bottles and paper napkins.

spender: in the summer of 1930 she took twenty-six friends to Paris: they were instructed to buy anything they liked and charge it to her. As time went on, she began to share Hearst's castle fantasies. Her Santa Monica Beach House, 'as big as a railway terminus', was an affair of white pillars (arranged round a marble swimming pool 110 feet long so that they were reflected in it) and vast rooms: her bedroom was so long that, to save her walking, she had a bathroom at each end of it. Rembrandts and Holbeins mingled with enormous paintings of Marion in her film roles. There were fifty-five bathrooms for 110 rooms. She and Hearst lived in the centre house to which four other houses were connected. These were partly for guests, but mostly for Marion's family – parents, sisters, aunts, uncles – and more than thirty servants. It took seventy-five woodworkers a year to carve the banisters of the main staircases. Whole rooms were brought bodily from old houses in Europe, three of them from a stately home in Ireland. Some forty fireplaces came from English manor houses. A Tudor inn from Surrey furnished Marion's wine bar. The only difficulty was that there wasn't quite enough land for a tennis court. The lot next door happened to belong to Will Rogers, who amused himself by refusing at first to sell. Hearst eventually paid him $105,000 for it, saying – and it was the motto of his life – 'Pleasure is what you can afford to pay for it.' He *enjoyed* paying too much for things: he would rather buy from Duveen at $200,000 than have the same thing from a smaller dealer at only $50,000. The Beach House cost $3¼ million, but the treasures in it were worth as much again.

It is not easy to keep track of all Hearst's houses. Very rarely did he buy anyone else's house: in 1929 he bought a house called 'St Joan' at Sands Point because, in addition to being turreted French Gothic in style, it had a real lighthouse next to it; and he gave $400,000 for 'Newcastle', the Long Island house of Mrs Perry Belmont (whom we know better as Alva Vanderbilt in her first marriage), chiefly because it had a moat with a drawbridge.

Wyntoon, Hearst's Northern California estate in a pine forest on the McCloud River 250 miles north of San Francisco, was a going concern when he bought it; but nobody was less dismayed when it burnt down and he could rebuild it. Now his fantasy took a new turn; for he rebuilt it as a Bavarian village, or rather a tourist's idea of a Bavarian village. There was, it is true, a castle called The Gables; and in a further weird reversion to childhood (if you can revert to something you have never really left) he built a chalet for himself called The Bear, and others called

Cinderella, Fairy House and Angel House, all painted, like Disneyland, with scenes from fairy tales. Hearst filled them with German antiques and cuckoo clocks, and walked about the estate in a Tyrolean hat, encouraging his guests to do likewise. There was room for sixty people in the guest houses, which were half a mile away from The Bear House, and life at Wyntoon appears to have been an endless party. Marion never liked it, and privately referred to it as Spittoon.

But the obsession with castles remained. Sooner or later he must have a *real* Norman castle. His magazines in England, *Good Housekeeping* and *Nash's*, were run by Miss Alice Head, who edited the first herself. In 1924 she was asked to find him a castle. She chose St Donat's on the South Wales coast, about seventeen miles west of Cardiff, standing in two square miles of parkland. This eleventh-century castle, in a remarkable state of preservation, she was able to pick up for £25,000. Hearst bought it after seeing a photograph of one room only. You might expect Hearst to dash across the Atlantic and look at it, either immediately before or immediately after securing it; but no, he did not do so until 1928. That summer he took Marion and a party of friends, including Miss Head, on a lightning tour of European castles, sometimes in hired cars, sometimes in horse-drawn carriages. They took in Italy, the South of France, the French châteaux. In Florence, Hearst's feeling for history found expression in a revealing phrase (and you have to imagine his high, weak voice saying it) – 'you just can't help feeling sentimental, can you?'

The climax of the trip, of course, was his first sight of St Donat's, where the party was joined by Sir Charles Allom, who had recently redecorated Buckingham Palace and was to advise Hearst on the redecoration of his castle. It was ten o'clock at night when they arrived, and there appeared to be no gas or electricity. Led by Hearst with a lantern, they were made to explore every one of the 135 rooms. To his delight, Hearst found he had bought a ghost as well: a certain Lady Stradling, who had lived there in the sixteenth century, was said to haunt some of the rooms.

Bathrooms first, dozens of them; then a banqueting hall designed by Allom, and much Jacobean panelling. Hearst's bedroom, all in red and lacquer, contained what was said to be Charles I's bed. A swimming pool, three tennis courts and a croquet lawn in the moat. Guests sat down to dinner knowing that the silver on the table, some of it Elizabethan, some by Cellini, was worth £50,000. One little snag: the Spanish cloister he had bought, which was stored in one of his warehouses in

Hearst with his sons in 1938 – four years before the great sell-up.

the Bronx, couldn't be fitted in. This was a pity, for he had bought it in 1926, sight unseen, in Segovia for a mere $40,000, though his expenses had been increased by demolishing it stone by stone, packing the pieces in more than 10,000 crates (which needed a special sawmill to provide the wood), and building twenty miles of track to connect up with the nearest railhead.

This did not discourage him from buying another cloister six years later. He found it in a Cistercian monastery in the province of Guadalajara, and this time chose cheaper forms of transport – mule, oxcart and ferry. The stones were then taken in twelve ships to San Francisco – why, it is not clear; for when they arrived Hearst did not seem to know what to do with them, and uncharacteristically gave them to a local museum which had neither money nor space to re-erect them.

The Depression was now on, and Hearst's accountants were worried. He was believed to have spent about $1 million a year on art treasures for the last forty years – one estimate puts this at twenty-five per cent of all *objets d'art* sold in the world during that time. How many things had he bought? Twenty thousand? All figures were guesswork. He himself certainly didn't know. His 'personal expenses' were put at $15 million a year, which was also the amount of his income. Therefore he was spending capital. Begged by his accountants not to spend so much on art and antiques, he was apt to reply: 'They keep sending

73

me these catalogues and I can't resist them.' The whole Hearst organization was now borrowing. In the Bronx warehouses and the San Simeon cellars lay the insides of churches and medieval halls, armour, tombs, tapestries, stained glass, Adam ceilings, statuettes of madonnas. The Bronx warehouses occupied two five-storey buildings. A staff of thirty included cataloguers, photographers, cabinet makers and an armourer.

It was immediately necessary to liquidate more than half of his publishing empire. This still left him with some thirty-five newspapers, twelve magazines, three radio stations and some mines, to say nothing of San Simeon, the Beach House, Wyntoon and St Donat's. Hearst's own salary was reduced to $300,000 a year, and for his 'personal expenses' he was forced to borrow a million dollars from Marion: he was pathetically grateful to her. Could he bear to sell San Simeon? Who could possibly buy it? For a time he contemplated building a smaller castle nearby, but was dissuaded. San Simeon was closed, and he and Marion lived for a time at Wyntoon. Together they watched Marion's old movies in the private cinema, and occasionally, it is said, *Citizen Kane*.

America was about to enter the Second World War: 1942 was not the best time to sell off the Hearst Collection, and most of his stuff fetched far less than he gave for it (he had anyway always overpaid for everything). The sale took place at, of all places, Gimbels store in New York, where only half the collection occupied the whole of the fifth floor. (The rest was still in the Bronx warehouses.) How do you sell a dismantled monastery? You don't. Hopefully, Gimbels offered 'easy payments'.

The treasures that he never parted with were the twelve full-length portraits of Marion in her film roles: they accompanied him and Marion to their last home in Beverly Hills. It should perhaps be recorded that Hearst, when he died in 1951, left $59½ million (his publishing empire had picked up considerably after the war) and a $43 million 'Foundation for Charitable Purposes'. Ten weeks after his death Marion married a captain in the merchant navy named Horace Brown. St Donat's had been requisitioned by the British Army in the war, and is now a school called Atlantic College. And San Simeon became a state historical monument. Monument to what? Aldous Huxley, in *After Many A Summer*, created a character named Joseph Stoyte, who also built a castle. 'That's his monument,' someone says, 'to a faulty pituitary.' The answer may be simpler. This was the child who had once asked his mother to buy him Windsor Castle – and the Louvre.

7

UNDESIRABLE RESIDENCE

'Why,' Alfred Krupp once asked, in what must have been a rhetorical question, since no one (with the possible exception of his doctor) would have dared to answer it, 'why can nobody stand me?' There were plenty of people, including one of the most beautiful women in America, who could stand William Randolph Hearst, with whom Krupp had two things in common: monumental castle-building, and a tendency to buy things when he was worried or feeling unwell, which was nearly always. Only Krupp seldom bought art treasures: he was more likely to buy companies, often without bothering to consult his colleagues – a Spanish iron ore company, ships, rival ironworks. Compared to Krupp, Hearst was almost cosy, his lack of single-mindedness a blessed relief.

The iron-souled Krupps grew with the war-hungry Hohenzollerns. It is difficult to imagine anyone being in love with a cannon foundry, but the first Alfred Krupp surely was, with a kind of spiritual joy which his atheism otherwise denied him. His guns and steamhammers and coalmines were his children as surely as his human progeny: he gave them family names – Bertha, Fritz, Amalie. So immersed was he in *die Firma* that he was forty-one when, in 1853, he married Bertha Eichoff. 'Where I thought I had only cast steel,' he said, attempting to describe his emotions, 'I found I had a heart.' It had never occurred to him to take a house a few miles away from the works: he needed, day and night, to hear machinery at work. So the bliss of the home

over whose threshold he bore his bride was qualified by smoke from the stacks, smuts suspended in foul air, fumes and films of sulphurous grease, seeping in at doors and windows and begriming her clothes and curtains. When the steamhammers fell, which they did at about the rate of a normal healthy pulse, the hundreds of Meissen ornaments and delicate wine-glasses on their shelves jumped and tinkled and sometimes shattered. And when, a year later, his son Friedrich was born, it was natural to name his newest, biggest steamhammer Fritz after him.

To the outside world, Krupps were 'merchants of death'. Alfred had progressed from three-powder muzzle-loaded guns, by way of that famous two-ton cast ingot at the Great Exhibition, to railroad rolling-stock (which of course would one day carry artillery), lighter howitzers and very heavy fieldguns. It was logical that a man who consumed so much steel and coal should safeguard his supplies by acquiring iron and coalmines. Soon after the mid-century he was employing some ten thousand people. To do him justice, he had given his workers the basic elements of 'social welfare', with housing estates, cooperative stores and bakeries, a factory health service, a relief fund, pensions, hospitals, old people's homes and a private life assurance scheme. If you worked for Krupps, you were secure for life – provided you did nothing which could be construed as disobedience or treachery. Bismarck studied the system; and so Germany had 'social security' long before Lloyd George, in the last years of Edward VII, introduced its first steps to Britain. But woe betide any Krupp worker who was a minute late for work: there was a severe system of fines for this and other offences. A squad of factory inspectors combed the great works for evidence of 'socialistic errors', paying particular attention to the trashcans, which were examined for liberal newspapers and 'used toilet-paper'. This last item may have some relevance to the fact that at Krupps, following time-and-motion studies, you had to have *written* permission from the foreman to go to the lavatory.

None of this seemed strange in the Germany of the 1860s and 1870s, where Krupps were seen as the embodiment of the Prussian virtues: honesty, hard work, accuracy, punctuality and reliability. What they were actually making was useful to the Fatherland (and also to the Fatherland's potential enemies), but nobody thought much about that: it was the ethos that counted.

This excellent reputation however was not enough for Alfred Krupp. He wanted to leave a monument to himself and his family. The family motto, *Cave Gryppen* ('beware of the Griffin'), showed a beast which was

Alfred Krupp listening to the sweet music of the steam hammers.

half eagle, half lion; certainly a beast of prey with the means of attack. It was possible for anti-Wagnerians to see a symbolism in Siegfried's sword Nothung, beaten out on the anvil of Germany, which was Krupps of Essen. Yet nothing of this was to be seen in the Krupp trademark, which was three interlocking wheels.

His monument, which should distinguish Alfred from all other 'chimney-stack barons' in Dortmund or Duisburg, Gelsenkirchen or Bochum, Kettwig or Mühlheim, must be a house. He owed it to his unique position in Germany: a Cannon King had to have a palace in which to entertain real monarchs, monarchs who would be his customers, the Kaiser's friends if not the Kaiser himself. Such a palace must

A family group to celebrate Krupps' 150th anniversary. Standing behind: Berthold, Klaus and Harald. Sitting: Waltraut, Bertha and Gustav, Alfred (the last sole owner of the works) and Irmgard.

not be entrusted to architects, who were forever bleating about 'practical considerations' and were generally wedded to particular trends – Palladian, Renaissance, neo-this and post-that. He, Alfred Krupp, would be truly creative: he would himself design his palace.

From 1865, for five long years, he made sketches. He started from a number of unusual assumptions. There must be no wooden beams or window-frames because wood was inflammable: all that was not stone must be steel. No gas, either: gas was dangerous: all lighting must be by candles in huge chandeliers and candelabra, with occasional assistance from oil lamps. All windows were to be sealed up: open windows caused draughts, and draughts led directly to colds, colds led to pneumonia and death. Besides, Alfred had invented an air-conditioning system of his own: all ventilation was to be by tubes. The building was to be in two parts: a vast, mainly Renaissance house made of limestone, with heavy square doorways and an iron roof, which some observers have compared to Cologne railway station; and another, smaller block to be known as 'the Little House', chiefly for the use of the family. The two were linked by a lower building which had almost no function but to connect. The all-important feature of the main building was the special suite on the second floor for the Kaiser and his staff when they came to stay.

But where to build such an edifice? It must be on a hill overlooking the River Ruhr, and the hill must have trees on it. It would be called the Villa Hügel, the Hill Villa. It must be close to the works, but it must not interfere with or be interfered with by the coalmine tunnels that ran in several directions underneath. No surveyor could really be trusted: Alfred would survey the district himself. He had in fact already decided on the site: it was a question of justifying his choice by science. He therefore built an extraordinary piece of equipment to his own design: an enormous wooden tower on wheels, so high that he could see over the top of trees. This was pushed and pulled around the smoke-laden countryside by teams of sweating workers, and ascended from time to time by Alfred in frock-coat and top-hat, scanning the horizon in all directions with a telescope.

Research confirmed his choice: never mind if the soil samples were not entirely satisfactory. The hill did indeed overlook the river, but unfortunately there were no trees on it. Plant saplings? No – it was now 1869, Alfred was fifty-seven, he might never live to see the full-grown trees. Why should not full-grown trees be transplanted? Each one would have to be dug out carefully and loaded on to a horse-drawn vehicle and then either dragged or rollered to its new site and be roped and craned into a vertical position. The Pyramids and Stonehenge gave scarcely more trouble. Nobody ever thought they would live, but they did. A forest had been moved from Gelsenkirchen and Kettwig to Essen, over distances of ten to fifteen miles.

Meanwhile Alfred had elaborated all his sketches: to the Renaissance exterior he had added fearsome gargoyles, strange animals in stone, lionesses with human female breasts, and large sculptured eyes that seemed to be watching visitors lest they should steal something or behave indecently in the gardens. He had originally budgeted 500,000 marks for the project, which (paid for out of company capital) was going to cost two million marks or more. Inside, he had multiplied the number of rooms so that many had no daylight. William Manchester, author of the leading book on the Krupp family, once tried to count them. He had been told by the Krupp archivist that there were 156 rooms in the main building, and sixty in the Little House. Manchester, allowing for the fact that every visitor left to his own devices got lost and wandered through some of the same rooms without recognizing that he had been there before, made the total three hundred, give or take a few secret passages and inaccessible rooms with secret doors. Alfred's bedroom was to have three locked doors to protect him (against what? we may guess, but we do not know). And Alfred's study was to be directly over the stables, for there was a medical belief at the time that the ammoniac fumes of horse-dung were good for the lungs, and the fumes were conveyed to him by special ducts. There was no evidence that Alfred was tubercular, but he was a lifelong hypochondriac, by no means a man to be left alone with a medical dictionary, and could imagine he had every disease to which people of his station in life were prone.

His wife Bertha was also hypochrondriacal, and made this one of her excuses for seldom being present while Alfred was building his Villa. She and young Fritz were always stealing away when Alfred was entertaining his 'crowned heads' and big customers. In this they were unlike their American counterparts, for it was usually the Vanderbilt and Astor *husbands* who ran away to their yachts while their fearsome wives gave parties.

In April 1870 – not the most propitious year for embarking on great buildings anywhere near the Franco-German frontier – Alfred laid the foundation-stone of the Villa Hügel. At once the wrath of the gods struck the enterprise. A stormy spring blew down the scaffolding; torrential rains waterlogged the foundations, for the earth was very soft, and such stones as had been laid sank and cracks appeared.

Most of those stones came from limestone quarries at Chantilly in France, and French stonemasons were at Essen erecting them. Alfred must have foreseen the war that broke out between France and Germany in July 1870, but he does not seem to have foreseen any of its consequences, probably because he could not imagine that it would be anything but a walkover for Germany. The man who had provided the artillery for the German army now, in mid-war, strangely altered his priorities. The Villa Hügel must go on, whatever happened, *even if it meant using men from the Krupp works.* For some months the supply of limestone was unaffected, for by a small detour it could enter Germany through neutral Belgium. About the French stonemasons there was no problem: they went on building the Villa Hügel all through the war, and probably considered themselves better off than they would have been as *poilus*.

The nightmare of his life now was not that Germany would be defeated but that the Krupp works might be occupied and destroyed. If the French entered the Ruhr, he would not organize resistance to them: he would ask their senior officers to dinner, ply them with *Kalbsbraten* and wine, feed their armies too if necessary. By now Chantilly was cut off from Germany and Paris was under siege. Work on the Villa Hügel, which was still unroofed and only half-walled, almost stopped. As always when things became intolerable, Alfred wintered abroad. Usually he went to Nice, but Nice was now in France; and so instead he went to Torquay, taking the family with him. It was one of their last holidays together.

Torquay, or possibly the more relaxed atmosphere of England, did him good; but as soon as he was back at Essen he began to feel ill again. Moreover his bankers were needling him for overspending: the firm needed to borrow thirty million marks, which was difficult in the financial slump that had followed the war: what about the Rothschilds? Never, said Alfred; he would never be beholden to Jews. To add to his cares, he was having such frequent rows with the builders of the Villa Hügel, Messrs Funke and Schürenberg, who, to be fair, were trying to make the impossible possible, that his health was bound to suffer. He called in Prince Bismarck's own doctor, the very expensive Dr Schweninger, who looked the very model of a Prussian, monocle and all. Dr Schweninger, having handled Bismarck, could easily bully Alfred Krupp. He ordered him to get up at once, not smoke so many cigars, and cut down his drinking; above all to open the windows and let in some air, even the polluted air of the Ruhr. His scorn at the theory of horse-manure fumes was unprintable.

Alfred took none of his advice, obeyed none of his commands. The Villa Hügel, now an affair of honour, proceeded apace. He had his own railway station, his own branch line to connect the Villa with the rest of the steam-powered world. The Villa now resembled a royal castle, with its great spiked iron fence and its flagstaffs flying the Krupp griffin and the national flags of visiting royalty. Inside, all was discomfort: the central heating and air-duct systems never worked, the iron roof was too hot in summer and brutally cold in winter. It may be safely said that no guest ever had a good time at the Hügel. When you dined at the sixty-foot table in the dining hall, the food was lukewarm, and you were glared at, not by Old Masters, but by Prussian kings and kaisers in uniform with their sad-looking wives. If you risked a mild flirtation with someone else's wife, the butler would bring you a note from Alfred: 'A carriage is waiting at the door to take you to the station.' Other cross little notes, forbidding guests to do things, were pinned all over the house.

The Hügel became in fact – he said so himself – his prison. In 1882 Bertha left it for the last time: the last of their many quarrels had been about Fritz, who wanted to get married. The old man was left alone in the vast building with nobody but his servants to talk to. He was often laid up with rheumatism, and spent much time inventing bigger and madder guns (one of them could fire in two directions at once) and seeking ever-longer firing ranges: one, near Osnabrück, was more than ten miles long, and to get it he had to buy out some 120 small farms. If one of the great purposes of the Hügel had been to 'entertain crowned heads', he had certainly realized it. The Kaiser came four times: Grand Duke Michael of Russia was a guest and gave him a diamond ring; the Emperor Franz Joseph came and gave him a gold snuff-box; Li Hung-chang, called 'the Bismarck of China', stayed and brought the most valuable gift of all, a 2000-year-old vase. But Alfred now had nothing in life but the absorbing task of planning his own funeral. The Krupps always planned christenings, weddings and funerals like military operations, which indeed they resembled.

Young Fritz, despite his asthma and his precociously high blood pressure, which he tried to cure by gymnasium exercises, took over *Die Firma* from his father. He used the Hügel mainly for entertainment, attracting even more crowned heads than Alfred had done: Fritz got

Opera house? Office block? Museum? The Villa Hügel at Essen had
to be fit for a Kaiser to stay in.

on particularly well with the Kaiser. There were lavish business luncheons in Berlin, too, for 250 guests at a time, generally at the Hotel
Bristol, with Tyrolese yodelling, opera singers and black and white
minstrels: little model cannons on the tables had their muzzles stuffed
with violets.

Fritz spent little time at the Hügel: he had a shooting-box on the
Rhine, and another in Baden-Baden inherited by his wife Marga von
Ende. He had spent his youth wandering from spa to spa with his
mother; but in his early forties he started going to Capri. For his health?
well, yes; but there was a suppressed fantasy to be indulged. No Hügels
for him. He built himself a grotto on the south coast of the island in

Home was never like this. The draughty main hall of the Villa
Hügel has the world's third largest carpet. And Alfred's candles are
now electric bulbs.

a place so inaccessible that he had to make a private road (the Strada
Krupp) to get to it. Here was luxury even greater than that of Tiberius's
twelve villas, gardens full of terraced steps, flowers and statuary. You
could not enter the estate without one of Fritz's golden keys. It was
noticed by visitors to the island that certain comely young fishermen
and waiters had these keys. Why? Fritz said that he had built the grotto

84

for 'a secret brotherhood of mystics'. It was remembered that there were a number of waiters from Capri at Fritz's favourite Hotel Bristol in Berlin; and one of them wore a diamond ring Fritz had given him. Why Capri? because homosexuality was a crime in Germany but not in Italy. The Berlin police kept a dossier on Fritz and all other high-ranking homosexuals, but their findings were not published until 1919. The secret of the grotto might never have been known but for a Neapolitan newspaper which published photographs of alleged orgies there. The story was taken up in Berlin by the Social Democrat paper *Vorwärts* – and Fritz was finished. He 'died suddenly'. His poor health made this a possibility; but it may well have been suicide.

He had no son, but his daughter Bertha bore a well-respected family name, one after which huge guns could be called. A suitable husband was found for her in the person of a minor diplomat named Gustav von Bohlen und Halbach, who obligingly changed his surname to Krupp. It was as if old Alfred had been reborn. The Hügel came back into its own. Gustav spent and spent with apparently no other aim than to impress people with the wealth and might of the House of Krupp. He had Alfred's own mania for building: to the Villa Hügel he added turrets, moats, castellations: the general effect might be called Disneyfication. In his reign there were twenty-two cooks, more than a hundred servants and countless gardeners. Unlike Alfred, Gustav neither smoked nor drank, and was a fresh-air fiend: guests could not shut the windows even if they wanted to. The passion of his life was punctuality. His business luncheons at the Hügel lasted exactly twenty-five minutes, and heaven help slow eaters. On the third floor, in what was supposed to be a picture gallery, he had an electric model railway. He spent one hour a week there with his children, who were not allowed to touch anything, but *were* allowed to help make the timetables. For the time-tables, and punctuality, were all that mattered.

1919 was a bad year for Gustav: sentenced to a term of imprisonment by the French, who occupied the Ruhr after the First World War, he heard reports of French officers ordering his servants to shut windows and turn up the central heating. And when Hitler came to power, he was uncertain how to treat him. Bertha, who always referred to him as 'that certain gentleman', insisted that he should only be asked to dinner or tea: it would be sacrilege for a lance-corporal to occupy the Kaiser's old apartment. She nagged Gustav incessantly about the Nazi flags he flew outside, and the vast paintings of Hitler which he hung up inside. But there were no more crowned heads. And when, a few weeks before VE-Day in the Second World War, the Villa Hügel was surrounded by the 313th Regiment of the US 79th Division, who were received disdainfully by Dohrmann the butler, it was a simple matter to identify a tall, cool man as Alfred the Second, the new incumbent, and take him off to prison camp. After serving three years in prison as a war criminal, he built himself a fourteen-room bungalow in the grounds of the Hügel. He still had property worth £500 million, and a personal fortune of £90 million. The Villa, not inappropriately, housed the Coal Control Group of the occupying powers. It is now a stately home, open on Sundays. As Major General Matthew Bunker Ridgway, commanding the US 18th Airborne Corps, had said, on his first sight of the Villa Hügel in 1945: 'Future generations should see what I've just seen.'

8

DEEP IN THE HEART OF TEXAS

*T*hey say that Neiman-Marcus of Dallas, Texas, the store to end all stores, has no sense of humour. They also say that Neiman-Marcus could only exist in Texas. Are we to conclude that Texans have no sense of humour? Who, anyway, are 'they'? 'They' are Americans (envious Americans, we guess) from other states, especially other storekeepers. A sense of humour is only a sense of proportion, and if a state has so many millionaires that there is hardly anything to compare them with, and a way of life that Texans, at least, are quite certain is the best in the world, who's laughing? You can always tell a Texan, 'they' say, but you can't tell him much.

Since Neiman-Marcus is one of the features of Texas best known to non-Texans, let us get it out of the way with as few superlatives as they will allow. 'They' (in the person of Lucius Beebe) say that Neiman-Marcus spray their elevators with a special perfume to put people in a buying mood. As if they needed it: no Dallas lady could bear to be seen merely thriftily window-shopping. And this has been going on since 1907. One of the great Aunts of history, who would have interested P. G. Wodehouse, was Mrs Carrie Marcus Neiman, who, with her husband A. L. Neiman and her nephew Herbert Marcus, founded 'the Store' in a modest two-floor building. (Even today the store only has six storeys.) The Neiman-Marcus family were at this stage intelligently satisfying a new demand. On 10 January 1901, oil gushed from a 1160-foot-deep hole at Spindletop, near Beaumont, Texas, which had been drilled by one Pattillo Higgins and his engineer Anthony Lucas. Unfortunately they did not make big money out of it because their financiers in New York took the lion's cut. Beaumont is about 275 miles from Dallas, and the thought must have crossed the collective mind of the Neiman-Marcus family that a lot of Texans were going to grow extremely rich rather quickly, and would need to be shown how graciously to spend. Diamond Jim Brady had been a terrible example of enjoying money by simply chucking it around. A man or woman who is not used to spending money wants to know that he or she is buying the best, and for the best no price is too high. Joseph Duveen, peddling his Old Masters to anxious multimillionaires like Andrew Mellon, worked on the same principle.

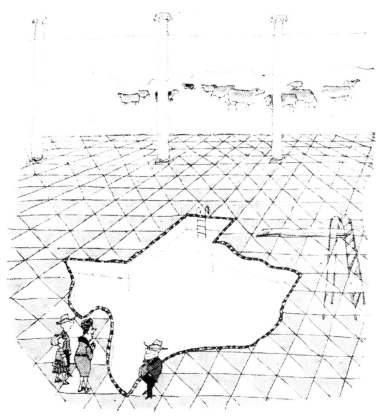

"Oh, you darling! You just knew I always wanted a Texas-shaped martini pool with a stuffed olive at the bottom!"

It's a large cup for a man who doesn't drink. Diamond Jim Brady, hero of many a twelve-course dinner, is presented with a trophy by J. Fred Zimmerman Jr at Delmonico's.

The legendary 'His 'n Her' aeroplanes 'for a husband or wife who's utterly impossible to buy for' were not a joke: they first appeared in the 1960 Christmas catalogue. Close observers of prices (not Texans) noticed that Hers cost a little more than His: but you could have both for $176,000. From here it is but a short step to His 'n Her Cadillacs (air-conditioned – but then, everything is in Texas, even hearses). You may not actually need an ermine dressing gown, but if you just plain want one, it will set you back $6500; or rather it would have done eleven years ago – I quote from the 1966 catalogue. As for ices flavoured with champagne (vintage Bollinger), Neiman-Marcus found it worthwhile to bring them all the way from Los Angeles, and it's no use telling them you'd rather have the vintage Bollinger by itself. A matchbox on which an Italian artist has painted an original miniature may well have sales potential. A telephone that plays music to your correspondent when you are called away seems less likely to appeal.

Aunt Carrie's descendant Stanley Marcus, the present incumbent, likes to think of himself as a Merchant Prince, and of the store as a 'magic land'. He would not like that word 'store', still less 'department store'. He has called it 'a collection of thirty-one separate but integrated specialty shops', and if ten words have to do the work of one, that is Neiman-Marcus luxury. Stanley Marcus sticks to the collection's first principle: that the rich need authority and standards set for them by experts, 'to avoid the pitfalls of the rich'. His advertisements for clothes use the phrase 'our stamp of fashion authority'. Less literate expressions include 'the Neiman-Marcus state of mind' and 'wantability'. You have to be a very young and rebellious and possibly poor Texan not to regard Neiman-Marcus as Olympus, where the Gods dwell.

Customers in thirty-nine countries of the world have charge-accounts at Neiman-Marcus (if you are a customer without a charge account, you're in a miserable minority of one to ten). But if they don't actually visit the store, they are missing a lot. Neiman-Marcus dearly love 'events', which are often 'expositions'. Their great fashion show of the year is in September, and it starts not in the store but in the grand ballroom of an hotel, generally the Sheraton-Dallas. Here, to music by the Dallas Symphony Orchestra, some forty models parade, some leading Afghan hounds (or even leopards); and the show usually ends with the presentation of Neiman-Marcus awards for 'services to fashion', which may be won either by a designer of the standing of Yves St Laurent or by one of Neiman-Marcus's best-dressed customers. Or it may be French Fortnight, with real French diplomats in attendance, and French celebrities of stage and screen. The whole first floor was once turned into a Hollywood-type set representing the Place de la Concorde, with real French cars and French policemen, while the Zodiac (the restaurant on the fifth floor, where the colour of the sugar always has to match the colour of the walls, which gives you fashion shows with most meals and is said happily to lose $50,000 a year) was transformed into Maxim's; and a special dish (not prepared by imported French chefs on the spot) was *flown in* every day from Maxim's in Paris. And when the opera comes to Dallas, Neiman-Marcus fashion advertising tells you what to wear for each opera: it goes without saying that you wouldn't wear the same dress for *Traviata* as for *Don Giovanni*, now would you? And Neiman-Marcus are not joking when they say in their catalogue: 'Many things may be had for under a million dollars.'

Texans are, to the eye at least, physically bigger than other people:

of their women a shrewd male observer has written that 'their legs sprout slimmer and their sweaters stick out farther' than those of other women. This is not easy to quantify with statistics, but a significant figure came to light during the Second World War, when rationing and restrictions hit the civilian population. The normal length of a ready-to-wear coffin in America is 6 ft 6 ins, and a regulation said that this must be reduced to 6 ft 3 ins. The Association of Texan Morticians protested that this simply would not do: Texans were *taller*.

Bigness, it follows, is not only desirable: it is unavoidable. So a Texas millionaire does not just have a handy little turboprop for getting away to his weekend retreat, or even an executive jet, but – in at least one case, that of Glenn McCarthy – a four-engined Stratocruiser, which cost Mr McCarthy $2 million and was only his *first* plane, the one he used for his family and his guests if they all felt like a trip to Canada for the fishing; not that there wasn't plenty of fishing much nearer. In the early 1950s it was chic, if you were in that class of plane-owner, to have an ex-RAF or USAAF pilot on your payroll, just as it used to be chic to have an English butler. The economics of running even a two-engined private plane in America in those post-war days were frightening: assuming an average of twenty airborne hours a month, what with fuel, oil, hangar, insurance and salaries of the crew, it cost

Charles Vanderbilt, megaphone in hand, supervises the moving of his private airplane.

about $45,000 a year to run, although over sixty per cent of this sum was allowable as a business expense. Today, there are fewer big-plane owners. Texas has been outdone by Saudi Arabia.

To be fair to the Lone Star State, it has always spent lavishly on public welfare and education, starting with the building of the Austin library in 1873 'to elevate the tone of our society', and at least twenty other states have a higher per-head income. But some heads are bigger than others. We must conclude that in Texas, money is for spending, and quality (and 'wantability') justify the price. Withal, there is still a touch of Jim Brady in many rich Texans: you cannot wear a lapel-button which says 'I've just given a million dollars to a hospital', but you can wear a whacking big diamond on your tie-clip. Sam Lard, who made three fortunes (in milk, beef cattle and finally oil) is said to have worn fairly conventional clothes (except for pink-and-blue boots), the sobriety of which showed to advantage the diamonds of his tie-pin and tie-clip, the diamond rings on his fingers, a large diamond brooch on his lapel, and – you did not see the full spendour until he sat down – a diamond-encrusted belt whose buckle was *all* diamonds. Mrs Potter Palmer had been outdone at last.

'Texas,' says John Bainbridge, the well-known Lone Star-watcher, 'is the only country where women wear jewellery at a fatstock show.' The claim to world fame of Mrs Robert Windfohr was the fact that she owned the President Vargas, the third biggest diamond in the world, worth $425,000 when it was found in 1938 and before it was cut into twenty-nine stones. It was sold to Mrs Windfohr by Harry Winston, the Duveen of the jewellery world. All this is considered vulgar by Hugh Roy Cullen – 'just plain common'. Cullen, a comparatively recent billionaire oil man from Houston who was at one time reputed to earn a million dollars *a day*, thought wealth should be advertised only by philanthropy. Money, like-minded Texans argue, is the root of all good.

Very little evidence can be found in Texas that the spending of money does not bring happiness. It is a better place than most to be a millionaire's wife. She is never hatless, seldom casual in dress. Even in summer, we are told, 'when the temperature drops below 90, out come the mink stoles'. She appears to believe that the best of everything still comes from Europe, and so it is hardly worth mentioning to one's friends that one is just back from a week's shopping in Paris or Rome. At a single ball in Fort Worth, a trained observer noted dresses by Balmain, Fontana and Marc Bohan. A Mrs Roy Woods used to travel everywhere, in the States and abroad, with a special van behind her car containing three changes of clothes a day, looked after by a French maid. Both men and women, conscious of the history of Texas and its role as the last survivor of the Wild West, are apt to wear cowboy clothes with beautiful boots; to this a very rich man may add a silver tie and alligator boots with jaguar fur round the top. You are never absolutely sure whether they are in fancy dress or not.

When Mr Robert V. King of Houston gave a Roman party, it is said that cowboy boots were clearly visible beneath the togas. When Jake Hamon, the oil millionaire, gave his annual fancy dress ball, his wife rode in on an elephant. The annual party, no expense spared, is a feature of uppercrust Texas life. It may be an Aloha feast, with everyone wearing leis and squatting on the floor to eat poi and coconut pudding and steamed yams, taking part in Hawaiian dances and singing ukulele songs. It may, if you have the space, be a party for 1500 or so guests who will dine and dance to two orchestras. It may be a wedding reception or debutante party, with a special 'producer' like Joseph Lambert the designer. The most spectacular Texas wedding since the War was probably that of financier James Kirksmith to oil heiress Nancy Ann Smith in 1957, for which a local golf club was transformed into an eighteenth-century garden. All the lighting was provided by 4000 candles, and two lines of candle-lanterns lit the way to the house. The floral display included 200 dozen camellias, 1100 lilies, 45 dozen gardenias, 1000 roses, flowering peach trees specially planted, and 350 servants were specially hired for the occasion – too bad the Kirksmiths were divorced three years later.

Many Texans entertain in country clubs, and here perhaps we may note the class structure of Texas upper society. There are clubs whose membership is limited by huge entrance fees and subscriptions (the Cipango in Dallas and the International in Houston are generally quoted in this category), but there are also clubs from which the wrong sort of millionaire is excluded. The Hesitation Club (I have so far been unable to discover why it is so named) and the Shakespeare Club, both for women only, are limited to one hundred and to sixty members respectively. The first insists that every member be nearly or distantly related to at least one other member: the second, founded as long ago as 1886, comes right out with it and says 'no oil people'. You are aristocracy if you become rich in banking, not in oil, and preferably before the second oil boom of the 1930s. For oil people there are country clubs whose membership fees are in the $15,000 bracket. Such a club may

include a nightclub with cabaret. One great advantage of belonging
to any sort of licensed club in Texas is that you can buy liquor there:
some parts of the state still have Prohibition, which is why the sight
of people entering hotels with bottles in paper bags is a familiar one,
and the Great Gatsby is still alive and well. Many wealthier Texans
do their more spectacular entertaining in country clubs. You just telephone. A thousand guests? No problem: the management, knowing
you'll hardly trouble to ask for an estimate of the cost, will devise everything for your pleasure.

Home entertaining depends on size of house. It helps to have a ranch,
like the late Amon Carter of Fort Worth, proprietor of the Fort Worth
Star-Telegram, much real estate and several radio stations, who gave
parties for up to a thousand people, whom he summoned to dinner
by charging round the farm on a horse firing two revolvers. (Most
Texans seem to have some kind of gun, and people give each other
guns as gifts. It was not thought particularly odd when the San Antonió
Symphony Orchestra, playing Ravel's *Bolero*, enriched the master's
score by adding a pistol shot at the climax of the great *crescendo*.)

But the visitor who hasn't been there before may be surprised by
the modesty of many residences. It is OK to wear lots of jewellery but
less OK to have an ostentatious house. A Dallas real estate man said to
be worth $500 million, Leo Corrigan, lived in a house that cost only
$40,000, with nine rooms and only two bathrooms. Jake Hamon the
oil millionaire was content with a $47,000 Colonial-style house.
Another oilman, Algar Meadows, built a Tudor-style house in only
five acres for $500,000 (twice the national average for millionaires'
houses, according to a *Fortune* survey of about fifteen years ago), which
is a lot for Texas but not in the old Robber Baron league; John D.
Rockefeller, John Bainbridge points out, spent this sum every year to
keep up his Tarrytown estate (7000 acres) on the Hudson River. H. L.
Hunt, the oil billionaire, favoured an exact replica of George Washington's house at Mount Vernon. Of course you may, if you are Texas-
rich, have several homes, like Clint Murchison (who coined the local
proverb 'Cash makes a man careless'). He lives in a twenty-five-room
house described as 'Dutch colonial', with eight bedrooms and a sort
of dormitory for his friends 'so we can talk oil all night'. The entire
floor-space is less than that set aside by a representative Vanderbilt for
his servants. (Texans have few servants – they tend to hire them,
shimmering butlers and all, for parties.) Mr Murchison also has a farm,
a 75,000 acre mountain ranch in Mexico (which he needs his private

aircraft to get to, since no main road goes anywhere near it), an hotel in La Jolla, California, and an island about a mile and a half long in the Gulf of Mexico.

You would not expect Mrs Robert Windfohr (she of the 'third biggest rock in the world') to live in an average millionaire's house: well, she does and she doesn't. She has the Pavilion, an enormous art-and-entertainment complex added to the main building, some rooms of which have the outer wall made entirely of glass. Here there are games rooms, a bar, a solarium and a picture gallery full of modern French paintings. Many Texas-rich collect pictures and sculpture: they are tax-deductible, of course, if you bequeath them to an art gallery or museum, while retaining the privilege of keeping them for your own pleasure until you die. There is at least one wine merchant in Texas who has been known to deliver bottles of liquor packaged in prints of French Impressionists. A Fort Worth oilman named Ted Weiner created that rare thing in Texas, a folly or fantasy to show off his modern sculpture, including several Henry Moores, all floodlit by night. Land-scaping a garden in Texas is not easy because the terrain is so flat: you must either dig or import tons of earth. Mr Weiner brought in some 2600 tons of rock, enough to make hills and waterfalls, with loud-speakers cunningly placed for playing stereo music while you admired the statuary. That the spirit of Texas lives on is clear from a report, in December 1976, that a financier (*not* an oilman) is building 'his own personal Sphinx' on his ranch. Only slightly smaller than the real thing, its inside will be hollowed out to make a playhouse for his children.

Buffet suppers and barbecues predominate in an almost servantless society, but this was not good enough for a hostess named Mrs Bruno Graf, who wished to give not only dinner parties but highly original dinner parties. Edward D. Stone was famous, among many things, as the architect of the American Embassy in New Delhi, a structure which gave an overall impression of light and air and water, and an absence of walls. He had also created an astonishing building for the 1958 Brussels fair, 'the world's largest free-span circular structure', 350 feet in diameter, whose roof was supported by slender pillars and cables and under very high tension. Both these buildings made ingenious use of reflections in water. The central feature of Mrs Graf's house was to be a *floating dining-room*. She also insisted upon marble floors every-where, hi-fi in all rooms, an indoor swimming pool, and aluminium gates covered with porcelain. You entered the house by way of the foyer, through some of the many walnut doors whose ivory handles were chased with gold, past walnut crisscross see-through partitions (not walls) until you reached a bridge across a subtly-lighted pool. This led to the *pièce de résistance*, the circular dining area which either floated, or seemed to float, on the water. There is no record of any guest actually being sea-sick, but it was apparently routine for diners to fall into the pool. However, we have already observed that Texans do have a sense of humour: the Grafs, most thoughtful of hosts, had a supply of dry dinner-jackets and trousers for wet male guests (the women, it seems, never fell in).

We have not so far found many links, in the spending of fortunes, between Texas and the North, which is as it should be. Critics of the Lone Star State might say that Texans lack originality, and we might have to rebuff them with the example of Mr Everett de Golyer, of Dallas, who collects trains – railroad, not model ones – as a hobby. But just over twenty years ago there died, in Houston, a true eccentric spender who had an authentic touch of Diamond Jim Brady, but only a touch, for basically he was not generous. James M. West, known as 'Silver Dollar Jim', owned ranches and an unknown number of cars – eleven Cadillacs, thirty Oldsmobiles, and many more. One of the Cadillacs had four telephones, a radio transmitter-receiver, a supply of teargas bombs, pistols and a tommy-gun. This was because he had a hobby: he loved playing policeman, and was apparently allowed by the local police to do so. Nothing excited him so much as the wail of a squad car siren, and he invariably followed it in his own armed Cadillac. He does not seem to have had power of arrest, but he was never discouraged from pooping off with his pistols until one night he wounded not a criminal but a policeman. His other, meaner, kind of amusement, which earned him his soubriquet, was to carry never less than fifty silver dollars in his pocket, and throw a handful of them on the ground for the pleasure of watching the crowd scramble for them. When he died, his house was searched, and hidden in the basement was a cache of nearly 300,000 silver dollars.

9

TWO STOREKEEPERS

$\mathcal{L}$et Mother serve the eggs – her hands are smaller, and make the eggs look bigger.' This, the sound advice of a boy of fourteen already critical of his father's corner-shop sales methods, was uttered by Thomas Johnstone Lipton in 1864. His father was hurt, not to say shocked: he had saved for years, out of his £1.25 (S6) a week wage as timekeeper at a papermill, to buy his small business in Glasgow, and had no thought of expansion. He had already realized his ambition. His son should be honoured by being allowed to help him in the shop for twopence a week. In the fullness of time, he would retire, and young Tom would take over.

To young Tom that twopence a week was a goad in his flank. He would have his own shop, and that shop would beget another shop, and another. Shopkeeping – he could not yet express it in this way – was a branch of showbusiness. But first he had to get beyond two-pence a week. He became a cabin-boy on the Glasgow–Belfast run. He could not go to America while the Civil War was still on, but the moment General Lee surrendered at Appomattox Court House, he was off. He worked in a New England grocery store, drove a streetcar in New Orleans, travelled for a portrait firm, and worked on tobacco plantations in Virginia and South Carolina. Then, unlike his brother Scot Andrew Carnegie, unlike the New England Irish and the German Jews and the 'farm boys', he turned tail and went home to Scotland. He even sank his pride so far as to accept a job in his father's shop.

97

Left Sir Thomas Lipton (because he was 'in trade') never made the Royal Yacht Club till he was 81.
Right 'Tea Garden to Teapot': Sir Thomas cuts out the middle-man.

But in America he had learnt three principles: own your own sources of merchandise, sell cheaper, and *advertise*.

Two years later, in 1871, he had opened his own shop in Glasgow. He plastered his windows with comic posters and price tags; Glasgow thought them in bad taste, but came into the shop because of the competitive prices. He set up branches in Scotland, organizing stunt-publicity such as a parade of pigs dressed in kilts to advertise his good Scottish bacon. He imported 'the largest cheese in the world' from America (it weighed five tons) and tried to give it to Queen Victoria. He hid sovereigns in 'lucky pounds' of cheese and packets of tea.

By the age of twenty-nine he was a millionaire. The age of packeted blended tea, instead of an open bin from which the grocer shovelled tea into wrapping paper and laboriously parcelled it up, had arrived. But it wasn't enough to buy it wholesale. Lipton was now in a position to buy his own plantations. On a voyage to Australia he stopped off at Ceylon and bought some estates. Now he could sell his tea at only

1s 6d a pound, 6d cheaper than anyone else. Coffee and cocoa plantations followed: he had his own jam and bacon factories, fruit farms,
bakeries and hog-packing factories in Chicago.

It was time for an assault on the South. In 1894 he moved to London
and bought a sixty-acre estate called Osidge in Southgate, then an
almost rural suburb north of the capital. Here Lipton entertained parties
of 500 guests at a time, but they were usually his own staff. He had
not yet found his way into Society. He continued to advertise like mad,
claiming that Queen Victoria drank his tea. Apparently she did, for
in 1895 he was granted the Royal Warrant. Two years later he again
sailed to Ceylon on the *Oratava*, which, once safely through the Suez
Canal, ran aground in the Red Sea. It was the kind of cargo boat that
also took passengers. The only way to refloat her was to jettison the
cargo; and this was done, but not before Lipton had selected all the
bales most likely to float and painted upon them the words 'Drink Lipton's Tea'. This was curious behaviour for a man intent upon a knighthood; but the matter was clinched in Diamond Jubilee year, when he
gave £25,000 to the Princess of Wales's fund for the poor of London.
He was knighted at Osborne, where he was invited aboard the Royal
Yacht. Four years later, in 1902, he was made a baronet by his friend
Edward VII.

Yachts, indeed, were to be his passion for the rest of his life. He never
married or smoked and drank hardly at all, and his name was never
linked either scandalously or innocently with any woman in the Prince
of Wales's set, which he had now joined. Edward VII liked the new-
rich – not only because they were rich, but because they had become
rich by doing interesting things. Until 1894, when Sir William Har-
court equalized the death duties on real and personal property, rich men
had spent because they could. Now they began to spend to outwit the
Government. If higher taxation were on the way, then better spend
money while you have it. The new rich had not inherited land: they
might, however, buy it. Things were now going into reverse: the old
landowners had bought town houses to enjoy themselves in London;
but the new industrialist spent the proceeds of his City business on a
'place in the country' to relax in. The first had had dairy herds to feed
his children; the second 'went in for farming' first as a hobby, then
to make a tax loss. The influx of gold and diamonds from South Africa
meant a new kind of wealth, torn out of the earth (and out of other
men's hands) by adventurers like Barney Barnato. Why, then, should
not a multiple grocer get into Society? Society might say: 'What a

pity the King should take up with Lipton simply because he has made money.' But Society also knew that Lipton had rendered the King an indirect service by finding a job for poor George Keppel, husband of his mistress Alice, in Lipton's sideline, the Buyers' Association, which sold wholesale goods cheaply to its members. Moreover Edwardian Society spent a considerable proportion of its life in yachts, and Lipton had yachts.

His Mediterranean cruises just before the First World War, in his 1500-ton steam yacht *Erin*, were famous. Let America's Dorothy Dix describe this floating castle. She begins with the bedrooms (you do not talk about cabins on this kind of luxury yacht), which are 'little dens all done up in dainty lace and silk like a lady's boudoir' in which 'the washstands can be converted into desks' and the beds were gilt. She tried to count the clocks, antiques of ormolu and buhl, statuettes, the watercolours on the walls; noted that there were canaries in the music room and a harp on the hearthrug which nobody played. The dining room ran the whole length of the ship. Exquisite porcelain was everywhere, so that it was difficult to imagine an actual ocean voyage without fearful breakages. At night, three thousand electric lamps outlined taffrails and masts and rigging. Luncheon was often served on the starboard decks, which could accommodate seventy guests at a time. Whether you lunched or dined with Sir Thomas, you always got the same sweet – rice pudding: it was to him as treacle pudding was to Sir Philip Sassoon. But the great meal on board *Erin* (perhaps you had guessed) was tea, always served at 3 pm, 'with hot crumpets and broiled birds and champagne; and each guest was given a present'.

Erin's last cruise in 1914 was a climax in Lipton's social life. In the middle of it war broke out. He had started at Monte Carlo, then sailed to Greece. At Piraeus the King and Queen of the Hellenes came aboard, and were joined by the Grand Duchess George of Russia, Princes George and Alexander of Greece, and Princess Henry of Battenberg. The grocer, who because he was in trade would have to wait another seventeen years to be admitted to the Royal Yacht Club, was surrounded by Royalty. He sailed home and gave *Erin*, which had cost him £60,000, to the Admiralty.

In 1899 he had begun a thirty-one-year campaign to win the America's Cup for Britain. It was to cost him £1 million. He was up against J. P. Morgan, Cornelius and Harold Vanderbilt and their syndicates, whose money and expertise greatly exceeded his own. Over the years he became an heroic figure, his yachting cap a symbol of lonely

British obstinacy and a gift to caricaturists. He won other races, notably the King's Cup at Cowes in 1930; but the America's Cup always eluded him. This was strange, because it was almost thought of, even in America, as the Lipton Cup. All his racing yachts were called *Shamrock* (his parents had originally come to Glasgow from Co. Monaghan). There were five of them, all launched by Society ladies such as Lady Shaftesbury. *Shamrock IV* (1920) came within a narrow margin of beating Cornelius Vanderbilt III's *Resolute*; but no others did, and his last unsuccessful attempt in 1930, when he was eighty, brought him two rewards. The first was membership of the Royal Yacht Club in 1931, the year of his death – never before had the Club admitted anyone whose money had been made in trade. The second was American recognition of his sportsmanship in the shape of the Lipton Loving Cup Fund, got up by Will Rogers and Mayor Jimmy Walker to buy an 18-carat gold cup, 18 inches high, designed by Tiffany and dedicated to 'possibly the world's worst yacht builder, but absolutely the world's most cheerful loser'. Presenting it to Lipton, Will Rogers said: 'I love you, Sir Thomas, but I won't drink that damned tea.'

Among Lipton's closest friends were Sir Thomas Dewar and Gordon Selfridge. Selfridge always referred to the other two as Tom Tea and

Shamrock arrives in New York harbour for the 1899 America Cup. Lipton spent 31 years (and £1 million) as 'the world's most cheerful loser'.

'Profits,' said Gordon Selfridge, 'are not the only prize.' No, indeed –
he spent almost all he had.

Tom Whisky. Dewar does not qualify for inclusion among eccentric
spenders; but Selfridge is a case-history of a man who left his spending
a little too late. One of the great 'ifs' of history is what would have
happened if he had been half an inch taller. An errand boy at eleven,
delivering newspapers and bread, he had a consuming desire to join
the US Navy. But the minimum height for a sailor was 5 ft 9 in. and
Gordon Selfridge was 5 ft 8½ in. But for that half-inch it is not impossible that in 1898 there might have been a Captain Selfridge at the side
of Admiral Dewey in Manila to 'shoot the Spanish fleet into scrap-
iron'.

As it was, young Gordon, from Ripon, Wisconsin, found himself
earning $10 a week in the basement at Marshall Field's store in Chicago
and learning the Field code: respect the customer, make shopkeeping
as dignified as running a diocese, money back if not satisfied. Advertising: never say 'cheap' when you mean 'inexpensive': brilliant lighting
to glamorize merchandise. A commissionaire to greet you as you
entered the doors; a feeling of entering a cathedral or the Savoy Hotel,
a place to meet your friends and (Selfridge's own contribution to Marshall Field) have tea with them in the third-floor tea lounge. After a
quarter of a century in Chicago, having found time to marry Rose
Amelia Buckingham, debutante daughter of a real-estate magnate, Selfridge came to London in 1905.

Where should his own cathedral of commerce be situated? He found himself up against the building restrictions of a very old city. Why couldn't he build a store with a 450-foot tower, nearly 100 feet higher than St Paul's Cathedral? He took some of his problems to Sam Waring of Waring & Gillow, who said irritably: 'Do you want a shop or a bloody Greek temple?' Eventually, against all advice, Selfridge decided on what other shopkeepers then thought of as 'the dead end of Oxford Street'. His telephone number would have class and be easily remembered: Gerrard 1. His advertising would have class and be in *art nouveau* style. British labourers he found infernally slow, and the men who dug the foundations were spurred on by a military band specially hired to cheer them up – the first use in Britain of 'Music While You Work'.

It was snowing a blizzard when, with £36,000 worth of advertising, the store had its gala opening on 15 March 1909. Every other store in Oxford Street had its name over the door. Not so Selfridges: you could not possibly mistake that five-storey Parthenon of a structure for anything else. Selfridge's competitors, such as Marshall & Snelgrove, were by no means dismayed: he was after all bringing great crowds to dingy old Oxford Street. Everything he did was news: the biggest book department in London, a 'silence room' where you could rest from the labours of shopping, and a tea garden on the roof. When Blériot flew the Channel, his aeroplane was on view at Selfridges: 'Blériot and I,' Selfridge said, 'were changing the world, each in his own way.' For tourists, Selfridges was third on the list after Buckingham Palace and the Tower of London. For housewives, he was providing 'a community centre ... so much brighter than their homes'.

The Blériot trick was repeated in 1926, when Alan Cobham flew to Australia and back in his seaplane, which duly appeared at Selfridges. When Sir Henry Segrave touched 203 mph at Daytona Beach, his car appeared at Selfridges. So did Amy Johnson's Gipsy Moth after her Australian flight. Selfridge's window displays regularly caused pedestrian jams along the pavements of Oxford Street. While the Treaty of Versailles was being negotiated, they featured a replica of the Hall of Mirrors. Selfridge decided one day that his customers might like to see what £1 million worth of diamonds looked like without bothering to go to the Tower to goggle at the Crown Jewels; and so, to the combined anxiety of underwriters and police, they did. Selfridge's fashion shows used debutantes as models: they were paid £20 a week. His Election Night parties in the store (the last one was in 1935) were famous: he hired cabaret acts to entertain his hundreds of guests, Society and showbusiness, while waiting for the results. If you wanted to know when the next earthquake was going to occur, you telephoned the man in charge of the Selfridge seismograph. Why were the waitresses in Selfridge's restaurant the first ever to wear trousers? Partly for publicity, but more because Gordon had worked out that: 'A girl so clad can take nine more steps per minute than a girl in a skirt.' There were contract bridge contests at Selfridges. If you lost a trouser button while in the store, someone would sew it on for you without charge. Every detail was observed by Gordon Selfridge during his morning inspection, in top-hat and tail-coat, of the 230 departments of his store.

So far the story of Gordon Selfridge is one of showmanship applied to business. Where, then, is the megalomania, the overbalancing by which the breed is distinguished? Sometime in the mid-1920s a journalist dropped a hint: 'He's a genius from Monday to Friday. Weekends, he goes mad.' There was another Selfridge of whom the twenty million people who passed through his store every year knew little but what they might pick up by looking through the *Tatler* and reading between the lines. We can date the beginning of this new life from the death in May 1918 of his wife, who lay in state under a pile of three thousand roses at his country mansion on the Hampshire coast, Highcliffe Castle. When she was buried, one of the restraints on his life was removed; the other was the dominating influence of his mother, who did not die until February 1924, when she was ninety. Gone was the discipline that had made him a puritan. He was now in his late sixties. During the next ten years he spent more than two million pounds on – what? The point was, he did not have two million pounds. Regarded by the world, who could only judge by his spending, as a multimillionaire, he was only a millionaire. There is perhaps a special ecstasy in spending money you have not got; but did he know he had not got it?

He had rented (not owned) Highcliffe Castle, parts of which were fifteenth-century, with its magnificent view of the Isle of Wight, since 1916. The rent was £5000 a year. He had lived for some time in a house in Arlington Street which had once been the town residence of the Earl of Yarborough, and had filled it with Greek statuary and medieval Italian books. He had also rented Lansdowne House (also at £5000 a year, plus another four or five thousand a year to keep it up); this at a time when his income was only £40,000 a year. Here he gave vast parties and charity balls. He did not seem to notice that the great landowning families were leasing out their houses because of death duties and supertax, and that he was also liable.

Now he must do all the things millionaires are supposed to do – keep little actresses, own racehorses, charter aeroplanes to Le Touquet and the Riviera, play the tables at Monte Carlo and Deauville, where the casino was run by the famous Zographos 'Greek Syndicate'. He had never been a gambler before, though it amused him to make an occasional wager in business, like betting Woodman Burbidge, the boss of Harrods, that he would make the higher profits during the next year, 1917 – the loser to give the winner a model of his store in silver. He was also known to say impatiently from time to time: 'I'll bet you a Rolls-Royce that you're wrong.' One of his daughters was married to a Russian prince, another to a French count, and his son, having distinguished himself at Winchester and Cambridge, was being groomed for business. He felt the time had come to let himself rip, and he did.

Gaby Deslys was the type of French actress, not unlike Mistinguett, who bursts upon the eye in spectacular revues, always at the top of an infinite staircase, wearing a huge headdress of feathers and sequins and swishing a huge fan, also of feathers and sequins; and as she prances down to the footlights you know you are suddenly going to be treated to the sight of her legs, all of them, right up to her thighs. She had a partner named Harry Pilcer who danced well but was completely outblazed by Gaby. Gaby was reputed to be the mistress of King Manoel of Portugal, and gossip said that she charged Guards officers a fixed fee for the privilege of 'having supper with her'. Whether she was also the mistress of Gordon Selfridge we do not precisely know, but he bought a house for her in Kensington Gore and she could order anything she liked from Selfridges at his expense. She did not treat him well: waiting at the stage door in his car to take her to supper, he heard her say to the stage doorman: 'Let him wait!' Gaby liked diamonds and chinchilla: she even had chinchilla rugs.

It is probable that the Dolly Sisters gave him more fun for his money. Their real names were Jenny and Rosie Deutsch, they had black hair with fringes, and they came from Hungary. They hit London in 1920 in Albert de Courville's revue *Jigsaw* at the Hippodrome, and New York three years later, meanwhile appearing in Charles B. Cochran's revue *League of Notions*; and Jenny appeared solo in the cabaret at the Kit-Cat Club, which was where Selfridge first saw her. Selfridge was fond of squiring beautiful women, and it was sometimes said that he did it to publicize the store: certainly women as different as Pavlova, Isadora Duncan, and ex-Gaiety girl Rosie Boot, Marchioness of Headfort, were among his friends. But with Jenny Dolly it became serious. She too could help herself to anything at the store. He covered her with jewellery until she rivalled Mrs Potter Palmer and Caroline Astor; girls then wore dozens of bracelets up their arms, and Jenny's bracelets were all set in emeralds. He fed her with ice-cream, of which she was inordinately fond. Her chinchilla cape was valued at £4000. Can he really have spent £2 million on her, as rumour said? When we come to examine his finances, we shall have reason to doubt it. Certainly he was landed with her gambling debts, which included £40,000 lost in a single night at Deauville Casino. Jenny's system was simple: she kept her winnings, and Selfridge paid her debts.

The affair went on into the 1930s when Selfridge was in his seventies. When the Dolly Sisters were performing at the Casino de Paris, he had tins of ice-cream flown to her daily, and chicken pieces for her Pekinese dog. Thinking of retirement, Jenny wished to open a shop in the Champs Elysées. The central feature was a replica of her bedroom at her villa at Fontainebleau. There is no evidence that Selfridge paid for the villa, but he certainly paid for the shop, which was advertised as selling 'the most expensive things in the world'.

He had become the archetypal sugar-daddy. Two other stages of the millionaire's progress must be recorded. The ambition to own newspapers was almost gratified in 1922, when after the death of Northcliffe he was restrained by accountants from buying *The Times* as a first step towards 'a world chain of newspapers'. And the yacht? It was a steamer called *Conqueror*, skippered by a Captain Lloyd, and its upkeep cost £10,000 a year; but nobody can remember when, if ever, it left its mooring in Southampton Water.

The Dream Castle, then? Surely Highcliffe filled that role? But no. In Selfridge's office, where the portrait of Marshall Field stared down at him disapprovingly, stood an easel. On the easel were displayed plans of a Xanadu so fantastic that Hearst would have been put out of countenance. Selfridge had bought 700 acres on Hengistbury Head, near Highcliffe, but on the other side of Christchurch Harbour. His plan would necessitate a diversion of the main line from Waterloo to Bournemouth, but he was already negotiating about this with the London and South Western Railway. The name of Philip Tilden has not come down to us with quite the ring of Lutyens or Scott (though he had laid out Sir Philip Sassoon's gardens at Port Lympne), but he was the architect chosen to design a palace in a mixture of Gothic and Romanesque, which would have a cloister with a garden of several acres in

The Dolly Sisters: Selfridge apparently could tell which was which.
On Jenny, he spent £2 million.

the middle, an enclosed winter garden (rather like the one at Margate, but surrounded by lounges full of French tapestries), a theatre, an indoor swimming pool, several vast banqueting halls, and no fewer than 250 four-room apartments for guests. He had not been allowed to build a tower in Oxford Street, but he would have one at Hengistbury, and a dome too: it should be as high as St Paul's Cathedral. This was not to be merely a home: it was to be another Palais des Nations, a world cultural and scientific centre with 'studios, laboratories, observatories', with the most beautiful view in England from the roof. This edifice would stand for a thousand years and 'England would be proud to add it to her heritage'. This was Selfridge's bid for immortality: his name would rank in history with Alexander, Charlemagne, the Medicis. It would cost £3 million.

Fortunately the Midland Bank Ltd did not see these plans. His income from the store had risen from about £40,000 a year in the 1920s to £100,000 a year in the 1930s. The store's annual balance sheet tended to show a monotonous item of expenditure, usually about £150,000, called 'Managing Director's account', from which a wary shareholder might conclude that this was what he spent on entertainment. There were long arrears of income tax and a huge overdraft at the bank. So worried were the Midland Bank that they put a director of their own on Selfridge's board. Worse still, it was found that Selfridge had borrowed from the store itself. There was an embarrassing gambling debt of £100,000 to a French casino, though this was chicken-feed compared to his gambling losses, mainly on behalf of Jenny Dolly, over the past ten years. In those days casinos did not sue for what was still regarded as a 'debt of honour'. There was another method: they 'sold' the debt to a finance company which could use normally punitive devices for recovering the money with interest. To do the casino justice, they had reduced the debt to £14,000.

Selfridge's colleagues acted swiftly: it was now October 1939, the Second World War had started, he was eighty-three, and over twenty years his debt to the store had grown to £118,000. He must repay this immediately or resign. He was retired on a pension of £2000 a year, shared a small flat in Putney with his son-in-law, Prince Wiasemsky, sold his cars, went to the store by bus every day and sat in his office doing nothing. Just before his death in 1947, he was seen – so the unbearably sad story goes – queueing at the Carlton Cinema, Haymarket, to see an old movie with Jenny Dolly in it – Jenny, who had just committed suicide in Hollywood.

10

COME TO MY LITTLE PARTY

'The hostesses of the Twenties,' Mr Beverly Nichols tells us (and he should know, for he was there), 'were like great galleons, sailing the social seas with all flags flying and all guns manned, relentlessly pursuing their charted course – and not above indulging in a little piracy.' By that he means that they enticed away each other's chefs, butlers, gardeners, maids and celebrity guests. Many of them were also hostesses of the Thirties, and they were a new breed. They spent great sums of money on collecting people as others spend on collecting pictures, with the special difficulty that people can get away. Entertaining was still competitive, but not in the Astor-Vanderbilt sense. No question of who was *the* Lady Cunard, because there was only one. Yet rivalry there was: Syrie Maugham and Sybil Colefax, living in adjacent houses in Kings Road, Chelsea, were not above looking out of an upstairs window to see what celebrities were arriving next door.

Ladies Londonderry, Londesborough, Ribblesdale, either widowed or married to invisibly dim husbands, the first 'political', the third 'social' (and a former Mrs J.J. Astor IV); Ladies Bessborough, Ravensdale, Dalhousie. It was perhaps no longer possible for a 'political hostess' to decide the future of the Empire: Somerset Maugham remembered an age in which a hostess could say to a Prime Minister: 'We're agreed, then, that Freddie shall have India?' It was still possible for a hostess like Lady Astor to *think* (and have her enemies think) that

she was able to influence international affairs: or for Mrs Ronald Greville, of Polesden Lacey in Surrey, to believe that by peopling her house parties with ambassadors she was preserving the peace of nations. In the old, grand manner she did indeed claim that she had prevented Lord Lloyd from being made Viceroy of India. She was an Hon. but not a Lady: she had inherited a fortune from her father, John McEwan the brewer, and was wont to say, in her earthy Scots manner: 'I'm beerage, nor peerage.' She was not, as has been rumoured, the mistress of Edward VII: her connection with the Royal Family was traceable to her father, who, with Sir Ernest Cassel and many others, got Edward VII out of financial jams; and so one also met financiers among the ambassadors at Polesden Lacey or her town house at 16 Charles Street. She was also frequently descended upon for tea by Queen Mary, usually at about six hours' notice – just time to get the red carpet out. With Mrs Grace Vanderbilt she could, and did, say: 'One gets through so many red carpets in a season.'

How rich was Maggie Greville? Many people who went to her parties expected to be remembered in her will, and were not. There is reason to believe that in her lifetime she had been generous by stealth. 'I am going to leave my money to the rich,' she said. It was generally supposed that she had about £7 million, but when she died in 1942 and her will was published it turned out to be only £1,750,000. There were, of course, 60,000 Scottish brewery shares in McEwan and Youngers, and a number of bequests to godchildren. But she left her jewellery to the Queen (including a sapphire and diamond ring said to have belonged to Catherine the Great), £20,000 to Princess Margaret, £25,000 to the Queen of Spain, and £10,000 to Osbert Sitwell. Osbert Sitwell was fond of her, but his account of a house party at Polesden suggests that conversation there was limited to such observations as 'Cézanne wanted shooting!' and 'I think Bolshevism should be put down!'

The fragments of conversation which have survived from the parties at Emerald Cunard's are a little more edifying. It is her introductions that people remember. One was invited to luncheon at 4 Grosvenor Square for 1.30 pm, and had to wait, stomach rumbling with hunger, until two o'clock, when Emerald made her entrance: as she did so, a servant switched on the central chandelier of the white and gold drawing room. Then came the American voice labelling everybody: 'This is Lady Diana Cooper, the most beautiful woman in the world. This is Mr Winston Churchill, the greatest orator since John

Theresa, Lady Londonderry, by the London society photographer Downey.

Bright. This is Mr Michael Arlen, the only Armenian who hasn't been massacred.'

Society in the 1920s and 1930s opened its gates to a new meritocracy. If you had published a novel which had sold only 1200 copies you were liable to be summoned by one of the lion-collectors to meet, and be met by, those who were evaluating your future. Greatest of collectors was Sybil Colefax, who collected Artur Rubinstein, the Sitwells and Virginia Woolf, and even, for a short while, stole George Moore from Lady Cunard. There is a joke-story that she once gave a party 'to meet Jesus Christ', who was, of course, seated at dinner on his hostess's right hand.

Lady Cunard and Lady Juliette Trevor (right) in 1933.

These hostesses were not rich by Astor–Vanderbilt standards: Syrie Maugham earned a living decorating people's houses and kept an antique shop in Grosvenor Square. Sybil Colefax also did interior decoration, and in a successful year earned £2000 by it, all of which was spent on entertaining. Her main source of cash was her husband, Sir Arthur Colefax, K.C., until his death in 1936, when she had to sell her Chelsea home, Argyll House. Harold Nicolson's diaries give us some idea of the genuine brilliance of her parties, especially her 'great' dinner party soon after the accession of Edward VIII: 'Rubinstein started to play Chopin. More people drifted in – the Winston Churchills,

Madame de Polignac, Daisy Fellowes, Noël Coward, the Kenneth Clarks...' The King and Mrs Simpson, Thomas Lamont, Chairman of J. P. Morgan were there, and Lady Diana Cooper sat on the floor: this, in the King's presence, was thought too informal, but the atmosphere eased when Noël Coward sang 'Mad Dogs and Englishmen', which baffled Mme de Polignac but cheered up the King, who had been bored by Chopin almost to the point of leaving early.

But meanwhile there had swept into London an American hostess of the old school, uninhibited by any awe of the atmosphere around her, and exemplifying the rule that you can't crash Society in your own country but you certainly can abroad.

To a carpenter named Whitrock and his wife was born, in 1895, a daughter named Laura Mae. Laura Mae was not destined to spend very long in Waupaca, Wisconsin, the town of her birth: there was no society in Waupaca. We next find her at the Blackstone Hotel, Chicago, as a waitress: here she could at least watch Society, or something like it, eating. The hotel had a house physician named Duncan MacMartin, who took a fancy to her and married her. Laura Mae then discovered that general practitioners were not in Society either, so that when the roving eye of James Corrigan, of the Corrigan-McKinney Steel Company, came to rest upon her, she seized the opportunity to divorce Duncan and marry James. James started off on the right foot by giving her, as a wedding present, a $17,000 Rolls-Royce which was crewed by a chauffeur *and* a footman, a bit of Vanderbilt (and Stotesbury) magnificence which few millionaires affected. The Corrigans lived in Cleveland, Ohio; Cleveland had a sort of Society, but James, she realized, wasn't in it. She was no doubt pondering this when James, after a lifetime of hard work and fortune-building, obligingly died, leaving her an income of $800,000 a year.

It was 1927, when practically anyone could give a party (especially if there was good liquor) and you wouldn't necessarily know who were guests and who were gatecrashers. Yet Cleveland did not come to Mrs Corrigan. She moved to New York – it was the same story. Very well: she would risk everything and storm London. It worked: London in the late 1920s had few hostesses so lavish as Laura Corrigan; London was in a mood for being amused, and Laura did not mind people making fun of her behind her back and mocking her lack of education. She bought a large house in Grosvenor Square which, with her famous weakness for French Malapropisms, she called 'my little *ventre à terre*'. She revived the Vanderbilt custom of giving expensive presents to her guests (they were indeed a way of getting people to accept her invitations) – diamond-encrusted cigarette cases, bracelets and gold sock-suspenders.

If you asked the 'right' people to dinner, she reasoned, and you didn't actually know them, they would telephone each other to try and discover who else was going to be there, and if someone, possibly the hostess herself, started a rumour that Prince George had accepted an invitation, why, all else would follow and you would be *in*, and only desperately rude or snobbish guests would refuse to ask you back. Lady Diana Cooper was one of many people who responded quickly to Laura Corrigan's brash charm: her entertainment value was overwhelming. Of course, people told one another, only an American could get away with this sort of thing...

She gave instructions to her butler that *anyone* who came to the door was to be given a cocktail – the butcher's boy, the Duke of York, the dressmaker, other people's chauffeurs. She was capable of improvising a party by ordering the entire stock of Fortnum & Mason's delicatessen department to feed her friends. When Prince George came to dinner, which in the fullness of time he did, she welcomed him, not with a Royal curtsey, but by standing on her head; and this was standard procedure at all her parties. (Lady Mendl, we shall see, was also a head-stander.) And when Prince George eventually became Duke of Kent and married Princess Marina of Greece, Laura Corrigan sent her a $5000 mink coat as a wedding present.

Mrs Corrigan was now on the brink of becoming an international hostess as well. She had chartered a yacht for a Caribbean cruise for her friends, giving each of them $200 'spending money' at every port of call. The sterling crisis of 1931 found her at the Mocenigo Palace, Venice, which she had hired, following a trend started by the Venetians themselves before 1914 and revived by Cole Porter and others in the 1920s, apparently to celebrate the fact that, as Malcolm Muggeridge expressed it after the inspiring first night of *Cavalcade*, God had saved our Gracious Pound. (Deauville, too, was full that year, with a splendid array of people spending their convalescent pounds – Gordon Selfridge, the Aga Khan, Lady Eleanor Smith, Lady Lavery, Noël Coward and Charlie Chaplin.)

The Venice palazzo party was the result of the invasion of European aristocratic and wealthy industrial families by American dollar princesses, often with Elsa Maxwell organizing it. For four consecutive seasons, Cole Porter hired one of the great houses on the Grand Canal.

He had dreamed for years of doing this, and it was made possible in 1923 by the death of his maternal grandfather J. O. Cole, who left him $500,000 and an income of $100,000 a year (of which he was to lose nearly half in taxes), and some land near Cole's birthplace at Peru, Indiana. Grandfather Cole had made $7 million from coal and timber in West Virginia. Cole Porter's mother and other heirs prudently invested their legacies in stocks and shares, and were rewarded with the 1929 Crash. Cole simply spent his, in a manner which soon earned him his 'rich playboy' label.

His 1923 palazzo was the Barbaro; in 1924 it was the Papadopoli; in 1925, the Rezzonico, where an eighteenth-century Cardinal, afterwards Pope Clement XIII, had been born and Robert Browning had died. The Barbaro had nothing which could be described as a bathroom, but its discomfort, while rather deflating Linda Porter's enthusiasm, did not affect Cole's. They were received into Venice's international set by Princess di San Faustino, who had once been Jane Campbell of New Jersey, and was now a widow: her red hair, worn in the style of Mary, Queen of Scots, made a vivid contrast to her black mourning, which in no way hindered her leadership of her bright young people. The Porters had a speedboat for getting to and from the Lido.

At the Papadopoli, the visitors ranged from Artur Rubinstein to Sir Oswald and Lady Cynthia Mosley, from Grace Moore to the ubiquitous Lady Diana Cooper, taking in Irving Berlin, George Gershwin, Lady Cunard, Tallulah Bankhead, John Barrymore and Diaghilev. Diaghilev offered to present an al fresco ballet starring Serge Lifar and Lydia Sokolova for Cole Porter's guests if Cole could provide an orchestra, a large statue and other props, and 2500 candles among the trees to light the show. Three large statues were borrowed from a museum; a hundred or so gondoliers attended, dressed in black, red and gold; and it was found that more than 200,000 candles were needed. A thunderstorm the night before the ballet ruined the fireworks which had been placed in position as a grand finale, but otherwise the show was a resounding success.

The Ca' Rezzonico, an untouched piece of the eighteenth century, cost the Porters $4000 a month to rent. The expense was shared with Howard Sturges, an extremely rich alcoholic bachelor. This time Linda insisted on installing bathrooms and lavatories, removing them again when the lease expired. The trouble with the Rezzonico was that it really needed a thousand guests to fill it, otherwise people simply got lost in its vastness. The Porters overcame this difficulty by hiring gondoliers in eighteenth-century dress to stand around in every room holding candles, and inviting a separate guest list of local civil servants.

Guests were in fancy dress representing four different periods of the nineteenth century. Before the ball, Elsa Maxwell gave a dinner for the Porters at the Grand Hotel, and the guest-list was a cross-section of who was who in Venice: the Count and Countess Volpi (he, the king of Venetian big business, was Mussolini's financial adviser), the Duff Coopers, Jane di San Faustino, Countess Zoppola (who had begun life as Edith Mortimer), Lady Wimborne, Princess Edmond de Polignac (formerly Winnaretta Singer of the sewing-machine family, painter, pianist and friend of Proust), the Agnellis of Fiat automobiles, and Prince and Princess Faucigny-Lucinge. This was known as the Red and White Ball: the Porters had paper clothes of all kinds made in red and white, and piled them on tables. At midnight the guests were let loose upon them and seized any that took their fancy and put them on. They were then shepherded into the brilliantly lighted courtyard, where they watched a high-wire act, and eventually returned to the ballroom to dance.

Cole Porter, posing as the eternal bored playboy, got a kick out of a floating nightclub in Venice.

Venice in the eighteenth century had been full of this sort of thing, and more. The Porters however were charged by certain critics, notably Boris Kochno of the Russian Ballet, with vulgarity. From their viewpoint the worst thing Cole ever did was his floating nightclub, a vessel on which 150 people (by invitation only) could dine and dance to a Negro band. It made only one voyage, largely because, in the lagoon, it rocked so much that guests could neither eat nor dance. For Linda, its fatal fault was that it had no lavatories on board. Thenceforth it was moored, with something akin to blasphemy, alongside the church of Santa Maria della Salute.

The Depression was approaching and ostentation, unless excused by its being devoted to charitable ends, was going out. Cole Porter made hostile international headlines in Japan in 1930, when, impatient at the infrequency of Japanese trains, he hired a special train to take him and his friends (among them Monty Woolley) from Tokyo to Kyoto. There were other Venetian galas, given by other hosts, and one of the last was the Bestegui Ball at the Labia in August 1951. While protesting at the bad taste of giving this kind of party when Europe had not yet recovered from the devastation of war, other rich-rich people trampled over each other to get invitations; and those who were unlucky ostentatiously moved out of the Serene City.

'International Society' meant that at the highest level its members all knew each other and visited each other's houses on travels abroad. Thus Count Alfred Potocki, the Master of Lançut in Poland, knew or was related to all other nobility in Europe, stayed with the Maharaja of Bikaner in India, met Cole Porter at the Duke of Alba's in Spain, knew most of the Rothschilds. His visitors' book at Lançut was signed by Noël Coward and Gladys Vanderbilt (who had married his kinsman Count Szechenyi), the Duke and Duchess de Noailles, and – Laura Corrigan! When he went to London 'for the Season', he bought horses and clothes and cars: 'My London tailors made me suits by the dozen, shirtmakers shirts by the score ... Once I ordered three Rolls-Royces at the same time.' At Polesden Lacey he met the Aga Khan, the King and Queen of Siam and the Marconis. He visited Hearst at San Simeon, and in New York, at a dinner given by Mrs Edward T. Stotesbury, was delighted to meet a footman who had once worked for him at Lançut.

A word about Mrs Stotesbury. With Mrs John Hay Whitney and others she was one of the great New York hostesses of the Thirties, and in Depression times it was appropriate that many of her parties should have charitable objectives. She was forty-three when, in 1912, as Lucretia Roberts Cromwell, recently widowed, she met and married

Edward T. Stotesbury, a partner in the J. P. Morgan bank, who was twenty years her senior. Just as Boni de Castellane had said of his ex-wife Anna Gould: 'She'll never know how much I loved her for her money', so Mrs Stotesbury described her second marriage as 'the most profitable transaction I ever completed'. Disliking the name Lucretia, understandably, she rechristened herself Eva. Mr Stotesbury had three grown-up daughters and his wife had two sons and a daughter by her first marriage, who were always known, in the captions to Café Society photographs, as 'the stepchildren of E. T. Stotesbury the Philadelphia multimillionaire'.

The wedding, at which the bride was given away by her son, Tony, who was nearly twenty-three, took place at her first husband's 'summer palace' in New Hampshire; and among the guests were President and Mrs Taft, and Mr and Mrs J. P. Morgan. Mr Stotesbury's wedding presents to his wife, apart from $3 million in cash, were all jewellery, including a diamond tiara and countless ropes of pearls. When they went to Palm Beach for their honeymoon, they were almost never alone, because Eva, insisting on wearing most of her jewellery all the time, had to be accompanied everywhere by a private detective. The lavishness of E. T. Stotesbury was continued in Florida, for he now bought land by the sea where he planned to build a 'winter palace' for his bride: it would have Mediterranean-style gardens, a zoo and an ornate tea-house and it would be called El Mirasol.

Grandest of all Eva Stotesbury's many houses was Whitemarsh Hall in Pennsylvania. Entering it for the first time, Henry Ford murmured to his wife: 'It's instructive to see how the rich live!' He was in the home of a man who, on his eightieth birthday in 1929, announced at a dinner given in his honour: 'I have achieved my life's ambition ... I have just heard from my financial adviser that I am worth $100 million.' Whitemarsh Hall had cost $2 million to build and its 147 rooms were heated and lighted by its own generating plant. With its own refrigeration plant, telephone exchange, laundry, and tailor's shop, it could have withstood a siege of several years; and those within would never have lacked amusement, for there was a ballroom, a cinema and a huge library. Mrs Stotesbury's daughter Louise married, among others, General MacArthur, and her son Jimmy married, among others, Doris Duke. Her system for entertaining repays study. She employed a full-time dress designer, who also acted as her social secretary, keeping lists of guests and food served at various parties, so that nothing was ever repeated, nobody was ever given anything they were known to dislike, and nobody ever saw her wearing the same dress or the same jewellery. Jewellery, she said, should always be 'rotated'. This concern for the comfort of her guests was paralleled, but not equalled, by Mrs Joseph Davies, wife of the American Ambassador to Russia, who on a cruise offered her guests, after dinner, the choice of ten different flavours of chewing gum. It was of her 2300-ton yacht ('thirteen times heavier than the *Mayflower*') that Westbrook Pegler the columnist wrote: 'Even the lifeboats have lifeboats' (which is on a par with a British financier of the 1920s named Loewenstein, who mysteriously fell to his death from his private aircraft: of him it was said that 'even his valet has a valet').

Standing alone (often on her head) among international hostesses was Elsie de Wolfe, who became Lady Mendl. Nobody ever knew how old she was. Her long life spanned a girlhood presentation to Queen Victoria and a close friendship with the Duchess of Windsor, and at her death in 1950 she was generally thought to be eighty-nine. She had three utterly different careers. Abnormally thin and strikingly plain, she had yet, by the age of thirty, become a star on Broadway (Ethel Barrymore was once her understudy!). In any company, nobody ever said she was beautiful, but most people said she was the best-*dressed* woman in the room. From self-decoration to interior decoration: this stage ushered in her second career, which in the next twenty years brought her a million dollars. Her first decorating job was at the Colony Club, which she and her inseparable friend Bessie Marbury helped to found: against all prevailing vogues, she chose old-fashioned chintz. In 1904 she opened a decoration and antique shop in New York, Elsie de Wolfe Inc., first on 40th Street and afterwards on 5th Avenue. Like Syrie Maugham a quarter of a century later, she became a Duveen of antiques, on which she took a flat ten per cent commission. She decorated houses for J. Ogden Armour, Mrs Earl Dodge, Gary Cooper and Mrs Leo d'Erlanger in London: the hallmarks of her style were Venetian mirrors, black and white paint, and animal skins. Her leading Royal customer was Edward VIII, for whom she decorated three rooms at Fort Belvedere.

Decoration and entertaining were two careers that developed in parallel. They began in 1887, when she and Bessie Marbury took a house where Washington Irving had once lived, and gave Sunday tea parties for people of achievement as distinct from mere wealth – Sarah Bernhardt, Oscar Wilde and Edith Wharton. From the 1890s onwards, Elsie de Wolfe seemed to 'know everybody', and to have been present

'Little parties' of the 1920s: *above* New Year 1922 at the Auto Club – Father Neptune and Harlequins. *Right* As the clock strikes midnight at the Piccadilly Hotel, 1930. *Below* The 'Joy of Life' Ball, December 1929 – just after the Wall Street crash: Mrs Woolley-Hart and Mr Alec French as Cleopatra and Mark Anthony.

at many of the Astor and Vanderbilt functions, including the notorious Bradley-Martin costume ball. Elsie and Bessie were quick to spot novelties that were likely to enhance life, and so they made much of Vernon and Irene Castle just before the First World War, and may be said to have had a hand in launching the foxtrot.

Elsie was present at a $50,000 ball given at Sherry's, New York, in 1905 by one James Hazen Hyde for the great French actress Réjane. The whole restaurant had been decorated in the style of Versailles, with a reproduction, it need hardly be said, of the Hall of Mirrors. It may have been this that planted in Elsie's mind the idea of holding court at Versailles itself. But it was not to be for another ten years. Meanwhile (it seems to have started about 1910 when she was fifty) she had formed her lifelong habit of standing on her head and turning cartwheels at parties. She and Bessie, one so thin, the other so fat, looking, it was said, like the figure 10 when they stood together, now lived much of their lives in France, where Bessie became very friendly with Boni de Castellane and Robert de Montesquiou, who nicknamed the two spinsters Tanagra and Tonneau Gros.

There were multimillionaires who had built themselves 'exact replicas' of the Petit Trianon at Versailles, and others, like Hearst, who

Elsa Maxwell, 'darling fat girl', commanding a £50,000 cruise on Stavros Niarchos's luxury yacht *Achilleus*, 1955.

had wanted to buy it and take it stone by stone back to America. Only Elsie de Wolfe seems to have thought of buying it, restoring it and filling it with people and a gaiety it had hardly known since Marie Antoinette. The war was over, the Twenties were on, and Elsie de Wolfe was bent on making her own reputation as a 'monster of frivolity' and turning the Villa Trianon into a 'show place of the world'. In thirty years she spent most of her fortune on the Villa. There were dinner parties for two hundred guests, masked balls, parties at which Murder and Mah Jong were played. In the garden she built a new baroque music pavilion, used largely for jazz bands. She had besides

Carnival in Estoril: Lady Docker, as a Gainsborough lady, gets more streamers thrown at her than anyone else.

a Paris apartment, another at the Ritz, and a house on the Riviera. For all the frivolity, Elsie gathered politicians round her too; and it was from her house that several Allied statesmen went, that day in June 1919, to sign the Treaty of Versailles.

At the age of sixty-five, Elsie decided to marry for the first and only time. Her choice fell upon Sir Charles Mendl, press attaché to the British Embassy in Paris; and if British diplomacy had appeared stiff in the past, its dignity was punctured forever as Elsie entered receptions with either a handspring or a cartwheel, according to her mood or the colour of her hair, which was sometimes green.

One more hostess who was *sui generis*: Elsa Maxwell, Lady Mendl's and most other people's great friend, Noël Coward's 'darling fat girl', who spent so much more of other people's money than of her own. Others usually provided the money, which could be anything from $16,000 to $60,000; Elsa provided the ideas. In the 1920s she had been employed by the Prince of Monaco to publicize Monte Carlo as a *summer* resort at a fee of $6000 a year, and by the Italian Government to boost the Lido of Venice. Two of her own parties, both in the 1930s, have become folklore. The Pet Hates Party invited everyone to come as the person they most disliked: it seems to have been a success, with one flaw: most of the guests were anti-New Deal, and there were far too many Franklins and Eleanors. The other, at Cap Ferrat in 1938, has been enshrined in Noël Coward's 'I Went to a Marvellous Party', which mentions the guests by name as Grace, Laura, Cecil, Elsie – and we are left to assume that they all behaved just as he said they did.

Her rules for successful parties were quite ruthless. Women guests must be beautiful, beautifully dressed and with 'not too many brains': brains in Society embarrassed other people. Men must be good-looking, well-tailored, not too interested in their own wives, and good dancers. All guests must obey their hostess and play every game she orders them to. And 'I'd rather they didn't throw bottles out of the window.'

The Rothschild wedding (in 1857) of Baron Alphonse and Leonora, daughter of Lionel, at Gunnersbury. The breaking of the wine cup, symbol of 'blended joy and sorrow'.

11

THE SIGN OF THE RED SHIELD

*T*hey were bankers and scientists and playboys, they built dreadful houses and beautiful houses in five different countries, they hunted and shot and gave away vast sums of money. One of them spent a fortune on establishing the Jewish National Home without ever departing from the family belief that every member should identify himself with and give full loyalty to the country he lived in. In one sense they assimilated; in another they never did, for they were too international and too rich; like Royalty, cousins could find themselves on opposite sides in a war, and still, by being spread over countries and continents, could stabilize currencies when the war was over. Most of them thoroughly enjoyed their money; while some wanted to be, and became, barons, none fell into the trap (as certain American millionaires, such as William Waldorf Astor, did) of wanting to be accepted as landed aristocrats. Hardly any of them were, or wished to be, gentlemen of leisure, and those who weren't collecting beetles or butterflies, fleas or pictures or double-firsts at Cambridge, put on top hats or bowlers and worked at the bank.

If I speak of the Rothschilds in the past tense, it is not that they have lost their glamour, even if the present Lord Rothschild votes Labour and has been seen going to work on the Underground. But we are looking at the ways in which people spend their money, and while it was being said as long ago as 1919 that the Rothschilds were down to their last millions, the period before 'death and taxes' took their final toll could not be extended far beyond the Second World War.

It took 120 years for the Rothschilds to rise socially from the Judengasse in Frankfurt, where they had worn compulsory yellow stars on
their coats, to the position of having among them the first Jewish peer
of the British realm and several Jewish members of Parliament. The
nation had powerful reasons to be grateful to them. They had supplied
the Duke of Wellington with gold pieces to pay and feed his distressed
troops in Portugal and Spain: Nathan Rothschild had done this by buying £800,000 worth of gold from the East India Company and – dis-
trusting ships which might be sunk in Napoleon's continental blockade
– wangled a passport for his nineteen-year-old brother James to go
overland. Pretending (to deceive the French) that Britain was striving to prevent him from exporting gold, he sent James to Paris where
the money was changed into various currencies for Wellington to use
wherever he might be in Europe. Thus an 'escape line' for gold, administered by other Rothschild brothers, was established across France
under the very nose of the enemy. And in May 1814 it was the Rothschilds who raised the necessary £200,000 to put the future Louis XVIII
briefly on the throne of France. In the London offices of N. M. Rothschild & Sons Ltd, in New Court, St Swithin's Lane, there still hangs
a letter from the Treasury authorizing Nathan Rothschild to send gold
to Wellington in Spain, and a receipt for £2 million of the money.
In 1854 Nathan's son Lionel raised £16 million to finance the Crimean
War, while his uncle James underwrote 750 million francs for Britain's
unusual ally, France.

It seems to have been Nathan's widow, Hannah, who set her sons
building great houses. Her sons, she made up her mind, were too pale
and too fat. They spent far too much time in the office. They needed
exercise and fresh air. Riding would be good for them, and they might
as well have an objective: foxes. So she bought land in Buckinghamshire, to set an example. Soon after the Great Exhibition of 1851, two
of her sons bought estates near Aylesbury. Anthony (the first baronet)
bought a farmhouse which today is the Bell Inn at Aston Clinton: an
adequate country house for a banker of modest means. But the Rothschilds were now – for a few years at least – the richest family in the
world. Was not more expected of them? Anthony's younger brother
Mayer certainly thought so. After all, several Rothschilds were now
Barons, and barons must live in castles. So Mayer bought seven
hundred acres and proceeded to build the strangest, most ostentatious,
yet most fashionable palace in the land. He had recently been to the
Great Exhibition of 1851 in Hyde Park, which was afterwards dis-

mantled and reassembled at Sydenham, a suburb of south-east London, and popularly known as the Crystal Palace. Its architect, Joseph Paxton, had been superintendent of the Duke of Devonshire's gardens at Chatsworth, and so it was not surprising that he tended to see buildings as conservatories. He was also a self-educated botanist, who, having successfully cultivated the Amazonian lily *Victoria regia*, noted that its organic structure lent itself to design. Mayer Rothschild shared the opinion of Lothar Bucher, special correspondent of the *National Zeitung* in Germany, that 'the Crystal Palace is a revolution in architecture from which a new style will date ... it is a Midsummer Night's Dream seen in the clear light of midday'. Mayer must, and would, have such a palace of his own, based on the same materials, glass and iron, and marrying art to engineering.

The result was Paxton's Mentmore Towers, near Leighton Buzzard, still in existence and owned, until its sale in 1977, by the present Lord Rosebery. Krupp and Hearst would have approved; the Astors and the Vanderbilts might have felt it not sufficiently classical. The first reaction of almost everyone who saw the finished building, or even the plans, was stupefaction. Magnificence of this order had never been achieved even in those great northern estates the Dukeries. Moreover, everything worked, even the new-fangled central heating and 'artificial ventilation'. Outside, all was castellated grandeur, with towers and spires. From within, through plate-glass 'picture windows', one saw panoramic views of the Chiltern countryside. The enormous hall, lit by enormous gilded lanterns taken from the Bucentoro, the Doge of Venice's ceremonial barge, had a glass roof through which sunshine could beam down upon the black and white marble chimneypiece, nearly twice the height of a man, which had come from the Antwerp house of Peter Paul Rubens.

Almost every millionaire who furnished his house with antiques claimed that some of them had once belonged to Marie Antoinette: her fastidious person had certainly sat on some of Mayer's, for there was her monogram to prove it. There were, besides, French tapestries, Sèvres porcelain, and trinkets salvaged from the Ducal Palace in Venice, all of inestimable value.

The French Rothschild cousins did not wait for any of this: Baron James had only to see the plans to know that such a home was exactly what he too needed – only *his* palace must be twice as big. He too had a great estate at Ferrières in the Brie district about twenty-five miles east of Paris; he too commissioned a palace from the Duke of Devonshire's head gardener. Uncharacteristically, yet with an overriding new confidence, the Rothschilds began to compete with each other in spending. It was of Ferrières that William I of Prussia said: 'Kings could not afford this. It could only belong to a Rothschild.' He did not say he liked it. Neither did Napoleon III, who disliked the Rothschilds but needed money to finance a war. He was invited to Ferrières in February 1862 to hunt, shoot a thousand birds, plant a memorial cedar tree in the gardens, be waited on by liveried servants, eat off Sèvres porcelain, and be sung to by a choir from the Opéra while he did so; also to explore the lakes, conservatories, farm, riding school, bakery and dairy which were adjuncts to the estate. In vain: Emperor and Rothschilds

The foyer at Ferrières, Baron James's answer to Mentmore: 'Kings could not afford this.'

continued to dislike each other. The situation was perhaps complicated by the fact that Baron James's brothers Alphonse and Gustave shared a mistress, the Comtesse de Castiglione, who was also the mistress of Napoleon III. In general, the French Rothschilds much preferred entertaining the Prince of Wales, who had been at Cambridge with their English cousin Nathaniel, and through him had become friendly with his brothers Alfred and Leo and their Austrian cousin Ferdinand. The Prince was accused, in gossip and cartoon, of borrowing money from them all. There is no evidence that he did, but it is probable that they gave him useful tips on investment.

The Rothschild bank in London was now headed by Lionel, elder brother of Anthony and Mayer. He had a big town house at 148 Piccadilly; a country mansion which had once belonged to a daughter of George II at Acton, eight miles to the west, called Gunnersbury Park, inherited from his mother; and a small hunting box in Aylesbury Vale. At Gunnersbury he gave fêtes and entertained his great friend Disraeli (together they had bought the Suez Canal shares). Disraeli admired Lionel's landscaping, the subtle elegance of the lakes and flowerbeds, the winding paths and happily-placed pavilions and gazebos, and the famous Japanese gardens which drew from the Japanese Ambassador the famous comment: 'We have nothing like this in Japan.' 'A beautiful park and a villa worthy of an Italian prince,' Disraeli wrote. 'Military bands and beautiful grounds, temples and illuminated walks – all the world of grandeur present.'

In 1873 Lionel was sixty-five. Of all the brothers he had spent the most time incarcerated in the bank. He had embellished Gunnersbury, he had assembled an impressive collection of seventeenth-century Dutch and Flemish paintings, but he had not really *created* anything, he had left no monument. So Mayer had 700 acres at Mentmore? Very well, then – he would have 1400 acres; and this was the area of his Halton estate halfway between Wendover and Tring. To this he added Tring Park, a house designed by Sir Christopher Wren standing in another 4000 acres of land, which Charles II had given to Nell Gwynn: the initials NG were woven into the ceilings.

If Lionel intended to build a house twice as big as Mentmore, or even twice as big as Ferrières, on his Halton land, we know of no plans; nor had he time, for he had barely six more years to live. It was his son Alfred whose duty and pleasure it became to build the ugliest of all Rothschild houses here; and this was strange, because fair-haired Alfred, a lifelong bachelor, had the reputation of an aesthete. It cannot be pretended that he was of much use at the bank. He disliked all sports, even racing, and left them to his brother Leo. He specialized in French painting of the eighteenth century, dressed like a dandy, loved women. As part-owner of the Gaiety Theatre he numbered all the leading actresses and beauties of the day among his friends: by one of them

Lionel Rothschild, who financed the Crimean War, caricatured as 'the modern Croesus' in 1870. Disraeli's great friend and master of Gunnersbury Park.

he had a natural daughter, Almina Wombwell, who became Countess of Caernarvon. Dominating all was his passion for music.

For all his knowledge of French painting, he had, it was said, no visual taste. He had, perhaps, something in common with Philip Sassoon. Everything was overdone. 'Senseless and ill-applied magnificence... combination of a French château and a gambling house... lavish wealth thrust up your nose!... ghastly coarseness...' Visitors were brutally frank in their comments. Even the hospitality was overdone, peri-wigged servants pursuing guests with three flavours of tea and (so the anecdote goes) the choice of 'Jersey, Hereford or Shorthorn' cream; and loading them with fruit and flowers when they left to catch the train back to London at Tring station. Footmen with lanterns were posted all along the lanes so that nobody's carriage could lose the way.

Guests were entertained in a very real sense at Halton. In Alfred a ringmaster was struggling to get out. At his first house party in 1884, attended by the Prince of Wales and the Countess of Warwick among many other Society figures, he showed off his performing Japanese dogs. Soon he had a small private circus of his own in which the dogs, by now trained to jump through hoops, were joined by a team of ponies in drill formation, with Alfred, in blue frock-coat with a ringmaster's whip, directing everything himself. In much the same spirit, he formed his own orchestra at Halton and conducted it himself with a diamond-encrusted ivory baton.

For even the most ordinary weekend party, in the early years of the twentieth century, a special Rothschild train, upholstered in his racing colours of yellow and blue, left Baker Street station for Wendover. Waiting at Wendover were *two* cars, one of which had nothing to do but follow the other in case it broke down. Occasionally Sir Thomas Lipton was among the guests. He said nothing about the orchestra, hav-ing little ear for music, but was fascinated by the Sunday afternoon entertainment Alfred had planned. Guests were taken, in tiny carriages drawn by ponies with 'minute grooms in blue livery', to a chalet in the park to see a pack of blue-and-white King Charles spaniels. This was followed by a sumptuous tea, and finally by dinner, at which the speciality was *poussins haltonais* – young out-of-season pheasants which had been killed by wringing their necks.

In 1874, just after Lionel Rothschild had bought Tring but had not yet decided what to do with the 1400 acres at Halton, another Roth-schild had begun building an almost equally forbidding castle at Wad-desdon, six miles to the north-west of Aylesbury on what is now the

A41 road. This was Ferdinand Rothschild of Vienna, who had married Evelina, daughter of Lionel, and been left a widower at only twenty-six. Having taken British nationality at the time of his wedding, he planned to express his adoption of his wife's country by building – in Buckinghamshire, of course – a palace of his own. In no other way did he resemble Alfred Krupp; but for a man nurtured in the gentleness of Austria there was something very Prussian in the way he paused one day in the hunting field, set his eyes and his heart on a bare hill, and decided then and there to plant it with trees in the middle of which there was to be a house that should out-Rothschild all other Rothschild houses except Ferrières.

He bought 700 acres of land and proceeded to exert his will upon it. Of course it would be necessary to take the top of the hill off, to make a flat surface for the foundations. The house was to be of stone,

Lord Charles Montagu, Lord Stanley, and Mr James Rothschild, 1916

of course, in the style of certain French châteaux. The nearest point from which Bath stone could be carried was fourteen miles away, so there would have to be a special railway line built to haul it up. It all gave employment to several hundred workmen. And horses, too – oak, beeches, pines would have to be dragged from woods several miles away, and it took sixteen horses to shift each one. British draught horses were considered inadequate, and Percherons seventeen hands high and weighing 2000 lb each were brought over from Normandy. The telephone had but recently arrived in the neighbourhood, and the unfamiliar service was interrupted as telegraph poles were taken down so that the huge trees could be dragged along the road.

Baron James had borrowed an Englishman, Paxton, to design Ferrières. It seemed appropriate that Baron Ferdinand should borrow a French architect, Gabriel-Hippolyte Destailleur, to build what he saw as a French château. M. Destailleur was required to combine, in his design, the most impressive features of four different châteaux – Maintenon, Chambord, Anet and Blois. The fact that round turrets and tall chimneys, octagonal staircases and dormer windows do not necessarily blend (even if we call it Flamboyant Gothic) is neither here nor there, or rather it is here, there and everywhere. Waddesdon had seventy rooms.

Within, all was royal finery. Just as furniture sat on by Marie Antoinette appeals to millionaire collectors, so it is satisfying to be able to point to tables or secretaires, such as the black lacquer one in the Waddesdon morning room, and say: 'That was made for Catherine the Great.'

Lavish entertainment is a branch of showbusiness, and of course the show must go on. If you arrived at Waddesdon in a storm which beat down all the flowers visible from the house, you would find that they had all been replaced from the conservatories by breakfast time next morning. Wet or fine, some diversion had always been planned for you: Christy Minstrels, an orchestra, a famous singer. If you liked pictures and antiques, you could stay indoors for a fortnight and still find fresh wonders to feast the eyes. In the grounds were a small zoo and aviaries. And when Queen Victoria respectfully asked if she might call on Baron Ferdinand at Waddesdon in May 1890, her bath-chair was pulled round the estate by one of his spanking ponies. According to custom, she marked her visit by planting a Christmas tree near the house. She had already called on Ferdinand's sister Alice, who had a house in the South of France called Villa Victoria: Alice shared her brother's determination to make nature follow art, and had employed hundreds of workmen to make a new walled mountain road in three days, diverting a stream in the process, so that the Queen's entry to the Villa could avoid steep gradients.

One Sunday in July 1897, Arnold Bennett took a fancy to ride in a hansom cab through London before breakfast to see what happened in the early morning. In Piccadilly he noticed 'two Rothschild servants starting out for a bicycle ride'. How did he know they were Rothschild servants? Because in Piccadilly at the turn of the century they could hardly have been anyone else's. From Apsley House to Bond Street was a kind of Elysian ghetto, as Aylesbury Vale was an Arcadian one. In the 1880s, Rothschilds were to Piccadilly as Vanderbilts were to 5th Avenue. At 107 lived Hannah, one of the very few members of the family who had married a Christian, Lord Rosebery (though she did not change her religion). At 142 lived Alice, next door to her brother Ferdinand at 143. (Alice also had a house at Eyethorpe, near Waddesdon, so that she could be next door to her brother in the country as well.) At 148 Piccadilly, built by the first Lionel next door to the Duke of Wellington's Apsley House, lived Nathaniel Mayer, 'Natty', the first Lord Rothschild (his country house was Tring Park), famous for his caution. 'The way to make money is to sell too soon,' he used to say; and he refused to insure the *Titanic*, knowing nothing of ships, because it looked 'too big to float'. No. 148 was noted for its great ballroom, approached by a marble staircase, and its excessive use of scarlet and gold. Nearby, at No. 1 Seamore Place, lived Alfred, among exactly the kind of French eighteenth-century furniture and porcelain and gold clocks and enamel and mahogany that surrounded him at Halton. Yet there was one great difference: the drawing room, all in white, where Alfred engaged, at enormous fees, the greatest musicians of the day – Liszt, Melba, Adelina Patti – to entertain his guests. Seamore Place no longer exists: it was pulled down to make way for an extension of Curzon Street to Park Lane. At 19 Grosvenor Gate (also demolished) lived Louise after her husband Anthony died: she was a Montefiore, and for some years she had vied with Mrs Arthur Sassoon to give the most gorgeous dinner parties. At 5 Hamilton Place, parallel to Park Lane, lived Leo Rothschild, third son of the first Lionel: he also lived at Gunnersbury and one of the family hunting boxes at Ascott, near Leighton Buzzard. 5 Hamilton Place afterwards became a nightclub (the Milroy) and a restaurant (Les Ambassadeurs) at which people point out the banisters Edward VII, as Prince of Wales, used to love sliding down. Leo's invitation cards, around this time, tended to contain the words '. . . to have the honour of meeting their Royal Highnesses'. Leo also had a house at Newmarket, where he could indulge his passion for horseflesh: this was eventually to be complemented by an equal passion for motorcars – he became a founder-member of the Royal Automobile Club.

All bus drivers, conductors, cabmen and police officers knew exactly which Rothschilds lived where. At Christmas the drivers and conductors of London horse-buses wore the Rothschild racing colours because they knew that as they passed 143 Piccadilly they would receive a brace of pheasants from Baron Ferdinand, whose shooting parties had slaughtered so many thousands of birds that he did not know what to do with them. And if the Rothschilds got preferential treatment from the police, it might have been because Lord Natty encouraged his cook to offer free dinners below stairs to constables on the beat. And if you met a goat in Piccadilly, you knew that it was Alfred Rothschild's

Leopold de Rothschild at Gunnersbury.

harmless eccentricity to keep it as a pet, and if you took it home to Seamore Place you would probably be rewarded.

They shot pheasants at Ferrières, too; and even hunted stags, borrowing hounds from Tring so that English guests, among them the Prince of Wales, should feel at home. In the 1880s Baron Alphonse, son of James, who had married his cousin Leonora, daughter of Lionel, became almost as English as his wife, who introduced him – and her chef – to treacle pudding. In Paris they lived in Talleyrand's old house on the corner of the Place de la Concorde. Alphonse and his brother Edmond amassed splendid collections of medieval and Renaissance enamels and goldwork, and early engravings.

Another collecting Rothschild was Nathaniel (not Natty the Lord, but one of Natty's uncles), who, being semi-paralysed after an accident, emigrated to Paris in 1851. Two years later he did a thing no other Rothschild had yet done. Looking for a place in the country, he chose the gravelly slopes of the west bank of the Gironde around Bordeaux, 350 miles from Paris, for the excellent reason that it contained vineyards, in particular one known as Château Brane-Mouton, developed by the Baron de Brane, a viticulturalist of genius. Nathaniel, wine experts complain, 'vaingloriously insinuated' the Rothschild name, and was offended when in the famous classification of French wines in 1855 his vineyard was accorded only *second cru* status. The idea appealed to the competitive Baron James of Ferrières, who in 1868 paid 4½ million francs for the *premier*-est of all *crus*, Château Lafite, which has been described as 'so grand and sublime as to afford a symposium of the virtues of all other wines'. Poor James never fully enjoyed it, for he died a few months after the purchase. His youngest son Edmond, who poured £6 million into settling Jews in Palestine 'as an experiment', used technicians from Château Lafite to start Israel's wine industry. Lafite passed to his cousins Alphonse and Gustave, and eventually to a committee of Rothschilds. Château Mouton-Rothschild, used as an artillery headquarters by the German army in the Second World War, passed to Baron Philippe, who added other vineyards. Philippe, a poet and translator of English poets, founded and built up the famous 'museum of the grape' filled with *objets d'art* connected with wine.

Unlike fleas, the benefactions of the Rothschilds defy cataloguing; and the amiable eccentricities of what was once the richest family in the world have simmered down somewhat since 1914. The great houses in Piccadilly were sold. A new scientific spirit, at first playful, was symptomatic of the fact that fewer Rothschilds were going into the bank. Lionel Walter, second Lord Rothschild, had already begun it in the 1880s, collecting fleas and butterflies and eventually rare birds and animals. Going up to Cambridge, he took with him a flock of kiwis: it is not recorded where he kept them. He cultivated scientists and collected 300,000 different kinds of beetle. He took bear cubs to the bank, which was probably when his father first thought of disinheriting him. He drove down Piccadilly in a carriage drawn by zebras. This was the man to whom Arthur Balfour, Britain's Foreign Secretary, addressed the letter known as the 'Balfour Declaration' which 'viewed with favour ... the establishment in Palestine of a national home for the Jewish people'. He probably had more animals and insects named after him than anyone else. His collection of 280,000 bird skins now reposes in the American Museum of Natural History, New York City. He alone (but none of the banking Rothschilds) gets a complete article to himself in the Encyclopedia Britannica – as a scientist. His niece Miriam has succeeded him as what Lionel Walter would have called 'a professional bug-hunter': she took twenty years to produce an illustrated catalogue of her uncle's collection of 10,000 fleas.

In France, too, Rothschilds were somewhat losing their super-spending panache. They had their Paris houses and country mansions, stud farms and yachts, like other millionaires; and it is those who escaped from the bank who claim our attention. Baron Henri, grandson of Nathaniel, had (like the new proprietor of Château Mouton) moved to France after a riding accident and become a doctor of medicine, building two hospitals and dividing his time between his patients and motor-racing: in 1907 he raced against his cousin Lionel from Paris to Monte Carlo. When the First World War came, he designed motor ambulances for the Allied armies and invented a process for packing jam in tubes, like toothpaste; and in the pleasure-seeking 1920s he was seduced by the theatre, which he patronized in the typical Rothschild way: he built the Théâtre Pigalle and, under the name of André Pascal, wrote plays, some of which were performed there. Philippe, who inherited Château Mouton, also inherited the Pigalle. Of the Rothschild yachts we know little, but Henri's *Eros* deserves mention because of its human cargo – Henri sailed her round the Mediterranean full of beautiful women, most of whom were actresses. His cousin Maurice, a shrewd investor and the richest of all the French Rothschilds, was celebrated for the quantities of jewellery he gave to women he was not married to. Knowing this, Proust's friend, Robert de Montesquiou, tried to borrow some diamonds to wear at a fancy dress ball, but was given only a tiny brooch: 'Please take care of it, as it is a family piece.' 'I didn't know you had a family,' Montesquiou replied nastily. 'But I did think you had some jewels.'

There was, in Britain, one more magnificent Rothschild before the age of the Tube railway to work (in London) and the chauffeur-driven mini (in Paris). This was the second Lionel, son of Leo, who in the new twentieth-century Rothschild style combined fantasy with science. We have seen him racing early motorcars. He now discovered the delight of growing things. So far as we know, he was the first Rothschild to own a million rhododendrons, azaleas and camellias. The days of colonizing Buckinghamshire belonged to fifty years before. Lionel II broke entirely new ground when, in 1919, he bought 260 acres at Exbury, in the New Forest, opposite Buckler's Hard on the Beaulieu River. There were twenty senior gardeners and perhaps a hundred undergardeners who were accommodated in special cottages nearby. There was something of Waddesdon-Ferdinand about his engineer's approach to Exbury. He laid twenty-two miles of pipes to irrigate the land: it took 150 men ten years. A large part of the work was done at weekends under Lionel II's personal supervision. He too gave his name to plants he had bred himself, more than four hundred of them.

The trouble with rhododendrons is that they are in full bloom for only two months of the year. Nobody now lives in Exbury House, but visitors can go there on Easter Sundays from 2–7 pm. 'Large woodland garden of botanical interest,' says the guidebook. 'Tea: Montague Arms.'

12

BOADICEA FROM CAMBERWELL

---

*W*ith the possible exception of Laura Corrigan, we have not yet considered the art of becoming immensely rich by consistently marrying immensely rich people. But here we come to Fanny Lucy Radmall, born in the then leafy village of Camberwell, southeast London, in 1858. By a chain of events that neither she nor anybody else could have foreseen, she was destined to embark on a pattern of lavish expenditure that, against all reason, would ensure that in 1940 the Battle of Britain would be won, not by the German Air Force, but by the RAF. Commemorating the centenary of her birth in 1958, Marshal of the RAF Lord Tedder regretted that there was no monument to her on the white cliffs of Dover. It all goes to show that if money is spent in a good cause, you shouldn't look too closely where it comes from.

Fanny Lucy Radmall, who would one day become Lady Houston, grew up in the underworld fringe of late Victorian London. Her father made boxes somewhere in St Paul's Churchyard. Her mother? We know almost nothing about her. Lucy's account of her own youth was vague. Her father called her Poppy. She was the seventh child of a seventh child, which must mean something, even if it only makes you feel different. Having no education, she believed that education got you nowhere. What mattered was wealth and breeding and rank, the first two producing the last, unless you were Royal, which she admired above all else: Edward VII, and Edward VIII as Prince of Wales, she almost worshipped, and if there was one regret in her life it was probably that she was never the mistress of one or both of them.

By her own account, she began her career, sometime after the age of eleven, as an 'actress and ballet dancer'. Those who disliked her said this meant 'pantomime chorus'. In the 1870s she moved on the fringe of Evans's Supper Rooms, the Café Royal, Romano's in the Strand, the world of stage-door johnnies, elderly mashers and *cabinets privés* with champagne.

At sixteen, we find her in Paris, living with a brewer named Fred Gretton. We do not know exactly how long Fred lasted, but he was good enough to leave her £7000 a year for life. It is clear that Lucy had wise friends as well. It was the age of the *grande cocotte*, of Cora Pearl, La Belle Otéro and, just after the turn of the century, Gaby Deslys; and a certain Madame de Polès, known as a 'hostess' at her house in the Avenue d'Iéna. Mme de Polès had a friend called Baron de Braimond, a courier or intelligence agent for Rothschilds, who taught her how to invest her money, and Mme de Polès in turn taught Lucy. She taught her other things, too: that money was not of itself important, one simply needed to have enough of it; one might need it at any moment of the day, to gratify an impulse, and so it was best to have one's handbag full of notes or gold coins at all times. Mme de Polès found golden-haired Lucy promising material for the *demi-monde*, with her fashionable wasp waist and tiny feet (she took size 2 slippers, which don't hold more than a few teaspoonfuls of champagne); and she groomed her in much the same way as Colette's Gigi was groomed by Aunt Alicia.

Groomed her for what? Another period of obscurity sets in, and we do not know for certain how she got from Paris back to London. At twenty-five, in 1883, she married a man five years younger than herself, one Theodore Brinckman, who would one day be a baronet. This union lasted twelve years, and ended in divorce: circumstances unknown. Six more years went by, during which she seems to have dabbled in progressive movements of the Nineties, in particular Women's Suffrage. You would think, perhaps, that if she married again, she would marry a man of achievement or substance, a radical politician, a landed duke. But she was not yet, even at the age of forty-one, moving in the right circles. Believing men to be hopelessly weak, she chose the weakest of them; and so, in 1901, she married the 9th Lord Byron, known, for entirely guessable reasons, as 'Red-Nosed George'.

Lucy Houston: said Dewar
to Lipton: 'We must marry
her off, Tom!'

American tourists in Paris,
1879, around the time Lucy
was there.

They lived at Byron Cottage in Hampstead; but not exactly together, for he soon found himself banished to the servants' quarters which he seldom left, so terrified was he of meeting her and incurring her fury. It was at this period that Lucy was most aggressive in her support of the Suffragettes, shrieking 'Votes for Women!' at gatherings of any size at all, and buying hundreds of parrots, 615 of which she personally taught to say 'Votes for Women!' with the idea of returning them into circulation to carry out their propaganda work. She also, at this time, formed her lifelong habit of walking about Hampstead Heath, giving sovereigns, and afterwards pound notes, to anyone who either was, or looked, poor. Lord Byron was mercifully released from this life in 1917.

Being married to Red-Nosed George had by no means interrupted her search for millionaires. Gordon Selfridge was heavily married, but he had two friends, Sir Thomas Dewar and Sir Thomas Lipton ('Tom Whisky and Tom Tea') who, being bachelors of enormous wealth, were eligible. The whisky baron and the boating grocer, well aware of the danger, consulted one another: 'We must marry her off, Tom!' The year was 1918, and Lucy was sixty (but those who knew her said she didn't look a day over forty-two). What was needed was a millionaire about five years her senior. The two Toms craftily picked on a Liverpool shipowner named Sir Robert Paterson Houston, who was exactly sixty-five.

Houston was known as the Robber Baron. In the days before the Plimsoll line prevented ships from being dangerously overloaded (and also overinsured) he ran what were known as 'coffin ships' to South American ports. Lucy always swore that she saved him from ruin by advising him to sell his ships. 'Sir Robert,' she used to say in after years, 'always took my advice. That's the mark of a really big man!' But it took time – nearly six years – to hook him completely.

The love of Sir Robert's life, at this moment, was not Lucy but his 1600-ton yacht *Liberty*, commanded by his friend Captain Goodman, to whom he confided gloomily: 'Mark my words, Goodie – she's after my bloody money!' The *Liberty* had been built in about 1900 for Joseph Pulitzer, the American newspaper magnate, at a cost of $1,100,000 (£270,000). Among other modern conveniences, its cabins were completely sound-proofed. It cost £20,000 a year to run, and was a familiar sight in Cannes harbour, around the Seine estuary or in the Bay of Arcachon.

However, one thing in Lucy's favour was that Houston had recently

altered his will. He was a little touchy about his age, and his friend
Lord Birkenhead, famous as F. E. Smith the advocate, sharp-tongued
at the best of times, used to rag him about dyeing his beard 'with blue-
black ink'. He may or may not have known that he was down for £1
million in Houston's will – not that he needed the money – and he
made his little joke once too often. They quarrelled, and Birkenhead
was cut out of the will. £1 million going begging . . .

Lucy finally got Houston to the registry office in 1924. He had given
her, among many other presents, a £50,000 string of black pearls. It
was now clearly Houston's duty to remake his will so that Lucy (who
still enjoyed Fred Gretton's £7000 a year) should never starve. It
seemed easy and practical to switch Birkenhead's million to Lucy, and
this he did. Hell hath no fury like a woman unappreciated. 'But I
doubled your fortune for you!' she stormed, and tore the new will up.
He made a last will and testament leaving her between £6 and £7
million, and died two years later.

Lucy had achieved, at sixty-eight, one of her two ambitions. She
was a multimillionairess. It remained for her to realize the other: she
wanted to guide Britain, her troubled country, into – well, Noël
Coward's toast from *Cavalcade* will do – 'dignity and greatness and
peace again'.

It was clearly her duty to avoid as much taxation as possible, so that
she herself could control her resources for the best patriotic purposes.
For some time she had been spending part of each year in Jersey, where
there was no income tax. Jersey did not like her very much: there were
rumours that she had bribed a potato farmer, and possibly a Customs
official as well, to smuggle a quantity of jewellery from St Helier to
Southampton – could it have been worth the £146,000 that gossip said
it was? Jersey began to say quite freely that Lucy Houston was mad
and should be in a mental hospital. Her method of dealing with this
was to invite all the leading (and Royal) doctors of the day for the weekend and leave blank cheques on their dressing tables so that they could
name their fees. They were the great names of Harley Street in the
Twenties and Thirties – Lord Horder, Sir Arbuthnot Lane, Sir Farquhar
Buzzard. We do not know their diagnoses, and none of them was a judge
of mental illness; nor do we know the fees they charged, though Lucy's
staff estimated the cost of the weekend, including fares and expenses,
at £10,000.

Certain Socialist members of Parliament alleged that no death duties
had been paid on Sir Robert's estate, and that Lucy owed the Treasury

£3 million. Rubbish, said Lucy: she was domiciled in Jersey and there-fore not liable. However, she would make the Chancellor of the Exche-quer a personal gift of £1½ million because she admired him. He hap-pened to be Winston Churchill at the time, and she regarded him as the only wise and truly heroic politician of the day. He alone under-stood that Britain was in peril. She made out her cheque, and then asked him for a kiss, which he politely refused, calling her 'a modern Boadi-cea' and offering her a cup of tea instead.

Lucy Houston was no builder of Renaissance or Gothic palaces (for much of her later life she lived in a house in Portland Place with a butler, footmen and maids), and she had only two cars, a Rolls and a Buick, driven by a chauffeur named Foster. She loved to be driven at over 90 mph, shouting in ecstasy: 'Faster, Foster, faster!' The monument she wished her money to buy was unforgettable service to her country.

For some years she had been moving politically from the Right to the extreme Right, a fairly short distance in the early 1930s. The estate duty trouble fanned the flames of her hatred of the Left. One of her friends was Collin Brooks, editor of the anti-semitic review *Truth*. Her tiny griffon dog was called Benito because she admired Mussolini's cas-tor-oil treatment of Socialists. She now started an information bureau about prominent Socialists and all Labour MPs which would show that most of them were unpatriotic, few if any of them had fought in the Great War, and nearly all of them delighted in running down their own country. Some of these pamphlets were published by her own company, the Boswell Publishing Co. in Essex Street, off the Strand, under the general title of *Potted Biographies; A Dictionary of Anti-National Biography*. It remains a mystery why so few of her subjects brought libel actions against her.

Her secretary was a redoubtable Scotswoman named Bessie Ritchie. Houston was a Scottish name, and Lucy began to feel Scottish herself. Her hero at this time was a Scottish peer, Lord Sempill, whom she considered 'the bravest man in the world'. He had been a pilot in the old Royal Flying Corps and had a brilliant war record. Afterwards both the Japanese and the Greek governments had employed him to organize their Naval Air Services. He had then, like Amy Johnson, Bert Hinkler and others, tried to break the England–Australia air record in a light plane, crashed in a jungle and somehow survived on brackish water. He had attached a motorcycle engine to a glider and somehow flown to Sweden and back, only a few feet above the waves. He too was one of the heroes she would give anything to see running the country, with herself as a new Gloriana.

But the country was being run by Britain's first Labour Government, which was trying to deal with the Depression and the threatened end of sterling as an international currency. Lucy at once offered the Prime Minister, Ramsay MacDonald, £200,000 to be spent on the defence of London against enemy air attacks. MacDonald could not accept any sum of money with strings attached, and anyway defence always had a low priority in Labour policy. Lucy then tried the Chancellor of the Exchequer, Philip Snowden, with a gift of £46,000; she was prepared to admit that much income tax liability. In her covering letter (which, like all her letters, was scrawled in purple ink on mauve paper) she said: 'The Prime Minister may be too proud to accept my offer of £200,000 to defend London against bombs, but I hope *you* are not too proud to accept this cheque for the tax I should have paid had I lived in England.' He was not too proud; but he bought no warplanes with it.

Lucy was now spending a good deal of her time on her late husband's yacht *Liberty*, whose crew were fond of her (she gave them all £5 notes on her birthday). Her hatred of Ramsay MacDonald, when he became Prime Minister of the National Government in 1931, was such that she displayed, from end to end of *Liberty*, an electric sign in letters six feet high: 'TO HELL WITH RAMSAY MACDONALD'. This was followed up by a series of anti-MacDonald meetings, at some of which she announced, through a spokesman: 'I will give a reward of £5000 to anyone who can prove that Ramsay MacDonald took money from Russia during the last war for the purpose of fomenting strikes and revolution in this country.' These meetings were reinforced by showers of leaflets dispensed from the sky by Lady Houston's aeroplane, which flew low enough for everyone to see that it was painted over with Union Jacks.

It was inevitable that she should try to buy a newspaper. Fleet Street in 1932 was buzzing with rumours about it. The *Daily Mail* loved her for her stunt-publicity value, but – in the person of Oscar Pulvermacher, the night editor – warned her not to try for a daily paper. They knew she would want to write all the articles herself and that anything she touched would lose money. She did have a journalist on her payroll at this time, at the then handsome salary of £1200 a year. He was James Wentworth Day, famous for his 'countryman' articles and books, a man thoroughly at home with hunting, shooting, fishing, natural history and prospects for the Test Match. Mr Day wrote a biography of Lucy Houston to celebrate her centenary in 1958.

Failing to buy a newspaper, Lucy settled for a weekly review. The weekly review market – *New Statesman and Nation, Weekend Review,*

The RAF's 'Fairy Godmother'. Without her, no Spitfire.

Time & Tide, etc. – was overcrowded, and so she was able to pick up the *Saturday Review* for a mere £3000. It was too weak a publication to be worth amalgamating with any other. What she did to it has never been done to any magazine, before or since, with the possible exception of the satirical magazine *Private Eye.* The front cover carried a Union Jack and a Red Flag, with a caption: 'Under Which Flag?' The back cover carried an advertisement for a cold cure invented by Lady Houston herself. In four years she spent £70,000 on it. There was perhaps a hard core of fascist-minded readers who took it seriously; but the great majority of its 60,000 purchasers (she had raised its circulation to this figure from only 3000) bought it for uproarious amusement. Its newsbills became a feature of the London scene, every one of them attacking the Government in general or MacDonald in person: 'Our Navy Betrayed by the Lossiemouth Delilah!' and 'MacDonald Should Say Thank God for Lady Houston!' Occasionally W. H. Smith and other bookstalls, fearing libel actions, refused to stock the *Saturday Review*, whereupon Lucy organized distribution by street-sellers.

But this was the age of wireless: Lucy knew that the printed word was not enough. Sixty thousand copies of the *Saturday Review* would not penetrate the whole country. So she planned a private radio station whose sole purpose would be to broadcast day-long attacks on Ramsay MacDonald. It could not be on the mainland of Britain because of the BBC monopoly: it would have to be on a Channel Island. So she instructed her staff to buy one – Herm or Jethou would do quite nicely; and of course she would need a private aircraft to get to and from it. But the Government found legal ways and means of stopping her.

If, as Lucy believed, Britain was decadent, heroes must be encouraged ‚as well as recognized. Anybody whose name was in the papers after having rescued a cat from drowning or stood up to a bully could rely on her to send £5 'with Lady Houston's compliments and love'. One of them was a housewife who had punched a burglar's nose: 'Send her a fiver!' Lucy shouted to Miss Ritchie. 'She's got a bit of my spirit in her!' But for the higher heroism that promised the leadership Britain needed, one had to look among aristocrats. Lucy's adoration of Lord Sempill was now joined by her admiration for the Marquess of Clydesdale (afterwards Duke of Hamilton).

In 1933 no aircraft had flown much higher than 10,000 feet, and despite a brave attempt by Hugh Ruttledge's expedition in the same year, nobody had reached the top of Mount Everest. Why not combine the two? Lucy would provide the aircraft, a Westland Wapiti. She would also put up £100,000 to cover expenses, which, from her side, included publicity, such as the large banner which she had flown from the roof of the Grosvenor House Hotel. Two planes took off, one piloted by Lord Clydesdale, from an airstrip near Purnea, Bihar, zigzagged and circled and climbed, and cleared the 29,000 feet summit of Everest by 100 feet. The risk was greater than people knew at the time, because it was quite uncertain whether there was enough air at this altitude to support a heavier-than-air flying machine, and fog could have wrecked everything.

There were ovations and banquets and speeches, very fashionable in those times of national face-loss, about British grit and prestige. There was even – a great rarity – a special celebratory issue of stamps, though with George V's head on them, not Lucy's. Pope Pius XI, who had a scientific turn of mind, sent Lucy a personal blessing. Lucy, though flattered, thought it typical of Britain's decadence that the Archbishop of Canterbury had not done the same. And in Nepal a lake to the south of Mount Everest was named *Parvati Lal*, 'Lady of the Mountain', after her.

The 1935 General Election found Lucy interfering in all directions, paying people to create disturbances at meetings, and persecuting her pet hate of the moment, Sir Samuel Hoare, by sending 'black and white' minstrels, well supplied with alcoholic refreshment, to sing abusive songs outside Hoare's house in Hampstead, and a chant which went: 'We want no more of Samuel Hoare – he's not the man for Chelsea.' And when Stanley Baldwin succeeded MacDonald as Prime Minister, Lucy transferred most of her political attention to him. The famous letters in purple ink, sometimes six or eight pages long, poured through the mailbox at 10 Downing Street. She had written to Hitler saying: 'Join Britain in an alliance and together we will crush Russia!' She hoped Baldwin approved. She urged him to 'beware of the traitor MacDonald'. When these letters produced no result, she changed her tactics and tried flirtation. (She was seventy-seven and he sixty-eight.) Her weekly letters were accompanied by flowers – roses, carnations, lilies of the valley, £5 worth at a time – was there nothing beautiful that would melt him? He *must* fight Socialism more actively, he *must* rearm against Germany, he *must* get Britain out of the League of Nations ... Well, if he wouldn't answer her letters, would he please come to tea? To her fury, he sent Mrs Baldwin instead.

Now that, to her satisfaction, Sir Samuel Hoare had left the Foreign Office, she started work on his successor, Anthony Eden, the handsome, well-tailored white hope of the Tories whose whole political life was based on trying to make the League of Nations work. In a Commons speech he unwisely, and perhaps in genuine ignorance, asked: 'Who is Lady Houston?' That week's *Saturday Review* soon told him, in an article headlined: 'This Nancified Nonentity, Anthony Eden'.

Lucy Houston slept badly: she used to have nightmares about war.

After one of them, a vision so vivid that she felt she must do something about it instantly, she had dispatched her secretary Miss Ritchie on the choppy sea journey from Jersey to Weymouth with a cheque for £200,000 which she was to take to the Chancellor of the Exchequer, Neville Chamberlain – not at 11 Downing Street, where some Civil Servant would be sure to get hold of it, but to his house in Eaton Square. 'I want him to use the money to start a squadron of fighter planes to defend London. The Germans mean war ... It won't matter to Mr Chamberlain, the Chancellor and others in Paliament, because they can all send their families into the country when the bombs fall. It's the poor people I'm thinking of – the people who live in little terraced houses, the working classes. One bomb and down will come houses like packs of cards. Think of what will happen to the women and children then – trapped like rats under all those bricks and mortar. It makes me shudder...'

As we have seen, Chamberlain and MacDonald felt unable to accept the money. The interest of that letter is that she offered it for *fighters*, not bombers. Military thinking of the time was: 'Bombers will always get through any defences, therefore if we rearm we have to have more and better bombers than the enemy.'

But aircraft were getting faster and more manoeuvrable. Lucy Houston, in her ninety-nine per cent muddled mind, understood this. Among the several air races of the late 1920s, in which the latest planes could be demonstrated, was the great Schneider Trophy. It was flown over water, and all competing machines had floats underneath. Clearly a wheeled undercarriage and four or even eight machine-guns could convert such a plane into a fighter. By 1931, with Depression setting in and Britain facing the worst financial crisis of her history, participation in the Schneider Trophy had become too expensive for most nations. The Government had voted £17,500 a year to subsidize opera for five years, but now jibbed at providing £100,000 to finance an RAF entry for the Schneider Trophy. Lucy Houston, as soon as she heard this, wrote out a cheque.

The race had been won in 1922 by a seaplane designed by R.J. Mitchell of Supermarine Aviation, Southampton, in collaboration with Hubert Scott-Paine. Britain had competed seven times since 1914 and won four times. Without huge research grants, these races were the only way in which new high-speed aircraft could be developed. Mitchell-designed planes had won the Schneider Trophy in 1927 and 1929. Lucy Houston's offer gave the planemakers exactly six months to

149

produce their entry. Together Mitchell and Rolls-Royce came up with the Vickers Supermarine RR.S.1596. It was flown by Flight-Lieutenants Boothman and Stainforth; and Stainforth, attempting a world air speed record, reached 407.5 m.p.h.

Without this financial encouragement, there might never have been a Spitfire, which Mitchell produced a year before his death; or at least, there might never have been Spitfires in sufficient quantity to win the Battle of Britain. Its Rolls-Royce Merlin engine had been groomed for stardom by Lucy Houston's money. It was thus that Lucy earned the titles 'fairy godmother of the RAF' and 'The Woman who Won the War'. She was already a Dame of the British Empire, only the fifth woman ever to receive this honour (she had got it in 1917 for founding a rest home for nurses in the Great War). And she was the first woman ever to be invited to tea in the clubhouse of the Royal Yacht Squadron at Cowes.

The famous Spitfire.

But she did not live to see the triumph of the Spitfire. When Edward VIII ascended the throne, she looked to him as the new hero who would lead the nation back to greatness. In the *Saturday Review* she noted that instead of going to church on the first Sunday of his reign he had done some gardening at Fort Belvedere: an excellent example to the country, she thought – if everyone did more gardening Britain wouldn't be such a weak-kneed nation. And when the King announced his abdication, she was furious with him, or rather with the Communists, for obviously the whole thing was a Bolshevik plot. But when it was all over, she softened, and her leading article was headlined: 'Love Conquers All'. It was her last article.

When, on 29 December 1936, she died, singing a hymn, having, it was rumoured, been on hunger strike for an unknown reason, the windows of her sickroom wide open although her physician, Lord Horder, had insisted that they be closed, there was intense curiosity about her will. How much money had she left? To whom would she leave it? Was it true that Sir Oswald Mosley was down for £200,000? Was there a will at all? A clairvoyant said it was hidden under the floor somewhere in her house. For some reason, folklore has handed it down that there was no will. You only have to look up *The Times* of 4 April 1937: 'Dame Fanny Lucy Houston, D.B.E., of Beaufield, St Saviours, Jersey and of Hampstead, left £1,528,083.' She had made her will in 1930, leaving everything to her friend Miss Juliana Hoare, aunt of Sir Samuel Hoare, First Lord of the Admiralty, 'to do with as she in her great goodness of heart thinks best'. Unfortunately Miss Hoare had predeceased her by nearly ten months. So the will was administered by Lucy's sister, Mrs Florence Wrey.

Her jewellery was auctioned at Christie's in May 1937. It included a sapphire pendant formed of a large flawless stone with a cluster surround of fourteen diamonds 'formerly in the possession of a member of the Russian Imperial family'. The entire collection fetched £17,510.

The Times, for reasons of its own, said nothing about Camberwell. Lady Houston, it implied, had been born in St Margarets, Twickenham. Sir Theodore Brinckman, thrice-married gallant soldier, omitted her name from his *Who's Who* entry (he outlived her by five months). We are left wondering how much of Lucy's biography was her own invention.

'Free University education in Scotland' – with the help of £2 million
from Carnegie.

13

WEALTH AND STEALTH

---

*I*n June 1975 the late Paul Getty gave a luncheon at Sutton Place, his Tudor mansion in Surrey, for Nelson Rockefeller and members of his family, Mrs Henry Ford II, and Mr Carleton Smith. We do not know what they talked about, but philanthropy was probably on the agenda. For Carleton Smith was his adviser on philanthropy, and is still adviser to several other trusts and institutions charged with the disposal of very large sums of money – $70 million a year in one case – for the public good. 'My job,' Mr Smith, an American, has been quoted as saying, 'is spending other people's money.' Philanthropy, he says candidly, flourishes in America (or anywhere) because of the tax laws. Nearly all Mr Smith's clients, he says, beg him to keep their gifts secret.

We may therefore be unfair to rich men if we assume that, in the absence of evidence to the contrary, they are tight-fisted and do little for their fellow men and women. It is significant, perhaps, that Mr Smith, like the late Ivy Lee who persuaded the hated J. D. Rockefeller to give away his surplus wealth, was once in the public relations business.

Philanthropic trusts grow by investment and need whole staffs of people to administer them. In his lifetime John D. Rockefeller I gave away $750 million. (Some of it went to found the University of Chicago – on his own terms, which were that it should be 'aggressively Christian' with 'no infidel teachers'.) Between 1926 and his death in

1963 William Morris, Lord Nuffield, gave away more than £30 million, mainly for medical research and education. In the last eighteen years of his life, Andrew Carnegie gave away $350 million, also mostly for education, but including endearingly personal items such as 7689 church organs, 2811 libraries and $3,750,000 for the improvement of his native town of Dunfermline, Scotland. We need not take too literally his claim that: 'If I had my life over again, I'd be a $30 a week librarian,' but his Scottish respect for learning was genuine. He could have been America's first billionaire: instead, he was America's first great philanthropist. Henry Ford, not the most willing giver in his lifetime, was eighty-three in 1936 when the Ford Foundation was established. Nineteen years later it made the largest donation in the history of philanthropy – $500 million for more than 4000 'educational and other institutions'.

Henry Ford would not have given a damn; he might well have been enraged at the uses to which his money was being put. Despising all education except the vocational – 'reading musses up my mind' – disliking intellectuals, he had only allowed the Ford Foundation to get off the ground in order to evade death duties. (In 1935 Congress had passed an Act taxing inherited wealth at seventy per cent over $50 million.) He did indeed give away $36 million in the last thirty years of his life, but precious little of it to universities or libraries or art galleries. To the end of his life, like William Randolph Hearst, he regarded taxation as highway robbery.

Applying the inexorable test – did these men *enjoy* their wealth? Did they *enjoy* the results of their bounty? Did they have *fun* with their philanthropy, did they satisfy anything in themselves that could produce, however you define it, happiness? – we are forced to conclude that Ford and Rockefeller did not. Their children, the inheritors, were a different matter.

I do not quite believe Lucius Beebe's round assertion that: 'No Rockefeller in the record is ever known to have had a good time.' The idea of recreating colonial Williamsburg, conceived by the Rev. W. A. R. Goodwin, appealed to, and canalized, the castle-building instincts of John D. Rockefeller Jr in 1926. Over 3000 acres were acquired for landscaping, 700 modern buildings were torn down, there was no longer a single gas station to be seen, as an eighteenth-century town arose; the only example of a twentieth-century city being replaced by an historical one. I cannot believe that John D. Jr did not have fun doing it, or that he grudged the $62 million it eventually cost.

With the $451 million he distributed in just over forty years after 1917, he took in education, religion and historic buildings, including Versailles and several cathedrals: his interest in historic buildings was genuine. On the other hand, without being in the least interested in modern art, he gave more than $5¼ million to the Museum of Modern Art: an act of faith which he might have justified by his overall slogan, 'Giving is Investing'.

A critic of inherited wealth has lumped together Andrew Mellon, the banker, Joseph Duveen's best customer for Old Masters, with Rockefeller and Henry Ford as 'three small, cold billionaires'; yet Lucius Beebe, a friend of Mellon's son Paul, says he secretly gave away millions to unidentified good causes: he wasn't cold, he was just shy.

Those were the rich-rich; but the philanthropy of the merely rich may qualify for inclusion. To found an orchestra was a new departure in 1881, and it was done in Boston by a banker named Henry Lee Higginson, who actually liked music. The motives for collecting pictures are always mixed: we can seldom exclude greed and pride of possession, but the impulse is seen at its best when it is harnessed to the feeding of young artists. Nothing of this was to be seen in the life of Sir William Burrell, amasser of the biggest collection of paintings in Scotland – a collection that the general public has never seen: about 8000 pictures, tapestries and *objects d'art* believed to be worth £40 million. In 1944, just before he died in his late nineties, Sir William, a shipowner like Sir Robert Houston (only worse, because meaner – he somehow fed his crews on 1s 3d a day), presented his collection to the City of Glasgow. It was meant to be housed in Dougalston, his 360-acre estate six miles north of the city. Sir William had a morbid fear of fire, and a total distrust of fire-brigades: he would, therefore, hand over all responsibility to the City of Glasgow, which, at that point of the Second World War, with dockland fires enough and to spare, had other priorities and could hardly have been more embarrassed. There will one day, we are assured, be a Burrell Museum; meantime this weird mixture of oriental, French and medieval art is stored in a secret warehouse somewhere in the west of Scotland. Burrell has been called 'a millionaire magpie', 'a Balzac miser', 'a man who wanted to own the past'. He was perhaps Scotland's answer to William Randolph Hearst. In his extreme old age, almost blind, he would lovingly caress each possession, telling how he acquired it; and it seems that the deciding factor in each purchase was 'because someone else wanted it.'

This might have expressed the feelings of Calouste Gulbenkian, the oil emperor, had he begun collecting paintings earlier than he did. He seems to have started in 1895. He began by being fascinated by Guardi and architectural painting. He took advice (latterly from Sir Kenneth Clark of the National Gallery), studied, formed his own taste, specialized. The result, valued at £4½ million when he died in 1955, was 'the finest private collection in the world'. His pictures included Rembrandt, Reynolds, Lawrence, Gainsborough, Fragonard. Among his sculptures was Houdon's 'Diana', commissioned by Catherine the Great (but rejected by her as 'indecent'). He had Marie Antoinette's table, and the whole of J. P. Morgan's collection of ancient Greek gold coins ... All these were kept at his great house at 51 Avenue d'Iéna, Paris, with its extraordinary roof garden where real trees grew and golden pheasants strutted; a house, he told Kenneth Clark, 'built like a battleship, my friend', surrounded by burglar alarms and watchdogs. 'My pictures,' he said, 'are my children.' His collection certainly brought him pleasure, which he had not the slightest desire to share with anyone else until the late 1930s, when he allowed the best of his pictures to be shown at the National Gallery, so that, he said, 'the mob can have its stare.'

For the great Jewish families of New York, eighty or a hundred years ago, it was important to have good taste, but equally important 'to be inconspicuous'. The Vanderbilts might strut and spend, but if Jews did it they would be criticized. There was thus a powerful motive for *not* sharing your *objets d'art* with the public, for fear of attracting the charge of 'ostentation'. Buy good paintings and serious books, but don't wear 'flashy' clothes. Show your pictures only to a few friends ... The rules were not always obeyed.

Adolph Lewisohn (he who spent $300 a month on shaves and 'spent capital' during the Depression) combined taste with business acumen. In the private art gallery which occupied the top floor of his house at 881 Fifth Avenue he had paintings by Degas and Manet, two Renoirs, four Cézannes, some early Picassos; Rodin sculptures; and a Shakespeare First Folio and an illuminated Bible under glass cases. He had bought both Barbizon School and Impressionists before they were fashionable, and sold the Barbizons when they were at the top of the market. A Monet costing $300 in 1920 was worth thirty times as much by the end of the decade. Adolph has been described as 'a sort of Jewish Gatsby' who somehow reduced his personal fortune from $30 million to $3 million in the eight years before his death in 1938. His philanthropies, many of them secret, were enormous; like his son-in-law Felix

Warburg, he gave $1 million a time to charities. He was deeply interested in prison reform, and his hobby was prison visiting, especially the condemned cell at Sing Sing.

At 932 5th Avenue, in the 1880s, lived Jacob Schiff, banker and railroad man. One of the first wealthy New York Jews who broke the 'inconspicuousness' rule by having *two* summer residences, one in New Jersey, the other at Bar Harbor, Maine (to which, of course, he travelled by private rail car), he is believed to have given between fifty and a hundred million dollars away anonymously. 'Philanthropy', he said, 'should be done in a man's lifetime.' The Talmud was quite clear on the point: 'Thrice blessed is he who gives in secret.' He envied Felix Warburg, whose Gothic house at 1109 5th Avenue had, as well as a music room with an electric organ and a stained-glass conservatory, an Etching Room and a so-called Red Room full of Italian paintings, among them Raphael's 'Madonna and Child'. To this, Edward Warburg added a full-sized art gallery in 1908.

Opera, Henry James used to say, was important in New York because there was 'nothing else' – or nothing respectable – 'to go on to after dinner.' For many years Jews, among the few people likely to know a high B-flat from a triangle, were not admitted to the opera, where Mrs Astor and her friends and enemies paid up to $30,000 for a box, which had the owner's name engraved on a brass plate.

Otto Kahn, of Kuhn, Loeb the bankers, really knew about music. His family came from Mannheim, Germany, where, like the Warburgs, they had moved among artists, among them Clara Schumann. In the 1880s he had worked in the London branch of the Deutsche Bank, and, an unsuccessful playwright himself, had delighted in the company of actors like Irving and Tree and young Granville Barker, writers like Wells and Le Gallienne, and (through Sir Ernest Cassel) the Prince of Wales. With his dandified clothes, orchids and jewelled tiepins he slightly overstepped the 'conspicuousness' line; and in later years he was to buy far too many stately homes, one of which, however (in fourteen acres of Regent's Park, London), he turned into St Dunstan's hospital and training school for blind British veterans of the First World War.

When Kahn gave New York the Metropolitan Opera, he was giving it something he loved. He did, quite ruthlessly, the only thing a Jewish financier could do: he rescued the Met. by buying up more stock than anyone else, not caring whether he lost his money or not. It got him a seat on the Board and eventually an enormous, informed influence:

Opening night of the 61st season at the Metropolitan Opera, New York, 1944

it was he who knew which European conductors to hire, he who persuaded Toscanini over the Atlantic. He organized fund-raising, knowing that opera never 'pays'; but $2 million of his own money he was content never to see again. In his last years he became fascinated by (but did not enter) the Roman Catholic Church. It seemed to him that one of his many houses, in the Italian Renaissance style, would make a peaceful retreat for nuns, and he left it to the Convent of the Sacred Heart. It became known as the 'Otto Kahn-vent', and among its pupils was President Kennedy's daughter Caroline.

The Irish rich had their own pattern of hell-fearing philanthropy. Thomas Fortune Ryan, a Robber Baron if ever there was one, bought *two* houses next to one another on 5th Avenue: one to live and worship in (for he had a private chapel, of course), the other to convert into an art gallery containing mainly sculptures, three of them by Rodin, three of them of Ryan himself, with sundry busts, tapestries and Limoges enamels. With businesslike precision, but little generous impulse, he set aside ten per cent of his $200 million to give to the Catholic Church, for which Pope Pius X rewarded him by making his first wife Ida a Papal Countess. Ryan's smallest bequest, when his will was proved after his death in 1928, was to his son Allan, who, after trying to corner Stutz Bearcat automobile shares and generally offending the

Business Conduct Committee of the New York Stock Exchange, went bankrupt, owing $12 million. His son had defied him, and he did nothing to help him. He left him nothing but his white pearl shirt-studs.

The chronicler of the Irish-American rich-rich, Stephen Birmingham, has examined their social structure and found that there seems to be, at the very top, an 'Irishtocracy' led by the Papal Order of the Knights of Malta. There are said to be eight thousand of them in the world, and they have the right to telephone the Pope. They presumably include the Brady family, no relations to Diamond Jim but descended from Anthony N. Brady, partner of the celebrated Thomas E. Murray in such enterprises as the Albany Municipal Gas Company in the 1880s. In the 1920s his son Nicholas had two main residences, one on a large estate called Inisfada near Manhasset, Long Island, the other in Rome, the Casa del Sole on the Janiculum Hill, set in magnificent terraced gardens with fountains and avenues of cedars, commanding an incomparable view of the city. Nicholas and his wife Genevieve collected notable Catholics as other hostesses collected cabinet ministers or Surrealist painters. While giving several of their $100 millions to Catholic causes, they indulged their hobby of Cardinal- and even Pope-making. At the Casa del Sole guests met three Cardinals, Bonzano, Gaspari and Pacelli. At Inisfada guests met a young priest named Francis J. Spellman, who was chaplain in the Brady's private chapel. Soon he became a Monsignor, and a very few years later Archbishop of New York. Again, it was the lady who was honoured: Genevieve Brady became a Papal Duchess. And when Cardinal Pacelli visited America in 1936, Mrs Brady gave an enormous party for him at Inisfada. The eye-witness who said it was as luxurious as Clarence Mackay's famous 1924 reception for the Prince of Wales was perhaps exaggerating, but the future Pius XII drove through avenues of thousands of candles guttering in the breeze, and the house was piled with mountains of flowers as he entered to soft organ music.

Of the Astors, only one, Vincent, long before the guilty 1930s, actually *said* he 'wanted to do good' with his money. His father, J.J. Astor IV, who liked to be called 'Colonel', had gone down on the *Titanic*, yielding his place in the lifeboat to his young, pregnant wife Madeleine; when his body was recovered it was seen that he had managed to stuff $2,500 into his pockets. Vincent, aged twenty-one, inherited $69 million, an income of $10,000 a day, and his father's thirty cars.

When his father was drowned, young Vincent was actually driving one of those cars, which would have earned him a fearful scolding if

'The Astors built French châteaux' – like J. J. Astor's on Fifth Avenue

J.J. IV had survived, the more so because his passenger was Ina Claire, star of *The Quaker Girl*, with whom Vincent was boyishly in love. He had been driving his father's cars since he was eleven, but only under supervision: one of them was among J.J. IV's many inventions, a 'steam-driven Surrey'.

Lucy Kavaler, historian of the Astors, represents Vincent as a 'poor little rich boy' whose divorced parents had little time for him, and whose education was largely conducted by his tutor, H. V. Kaltenborn, who would one day become one of the greatest of radio news commentators. He 'had no *fun* with his money'. Didn't he? Jack Alexander, a writer who knew him in the years before the Second World War, gives the opposite impression. His 'fun' sometimes took the form of rather dreadful practical jokes, and he enjoyed simple pleasures available to everybody, such as 'Amos 'n Andy' on the radio, which he listened to at 7 p.m. (New York time) wherever he was all over the world.

'Poor' in the usual sense he certainly was before the *Titanic* went down. Even at Harvard he had been kept distressingly short of money; that is, there was none in his pocket, although if he ran up a bill, Father would pay it – the classically wrong way to bring up rich boys, or any child. Now, at twenty-one, this tall (6 ft 4 in.) ungainly, rather plain-looking youth became 'a sort of eligible American Prince of

Wales'. The first essential, the family felt, was to teach him the estate business, which he learnt under the instruction of Nicholas Biddle and his uncle, James Roosevelt, Franklin's half-brother.

'Doing good.' The Astor fortune has been built partly on owning slum property. Nobody could have called them conscientious landlords. The third J. J. Astor, who used to write 'Occupation: gentleman' after his name and said: 'Money brings me nothing but a certain dull anxiety', believed that: 'It is cheaper to lose a whole block of buildings by fire every once in a while than to pay insurance premiums.' Vincent's anxiety was about the Astors. Did they really know *what* they owned? Who was actually living in all those tenements, and what were they doing? Was it true that some of his lessees ran sweatshops, using private premises to evade the law? Vincent inspected them, and found that some of them contained brothels. This, he felt, was not only unsuitable to be associated with the Astor name, it was bad estate-management.

The do-gooding of Vincent Astor was always shrewd and combined with business reasoning. It would take time to get rid of tenement houses: it took him until the early 1930s, when he stopped owning them altogether. He now enjoyed a personal ring of confidence that was valuable in the property jungle: his real estate advertisements began with the words: 'Vincent Astor offers...' His father had been the great hotel-builder; but when Prohibition came, hotels became less profitable, so Vincent sold them, becoming instead a heavy investor who eventually sat on the boards of ten corporations. In 1914 when he was twenty-three, it was clear to Upton Sinclair the Socialist novelist that Vincent, who was already proving himself a conscientious landlord, was material for conversion. But Vincent would be radical in his own way and at his own speed: he would join no political party. When he got married, it was to Helen Dinsmore Huntington, the first of his three wives, very much out of the same drawer as himself. (This indeed may have been all they had in common. She was a generous patroness of music: he was tone-deaf.) Yet, when menaced with taxation (he was allowed to keep $813,000 out of his annual income of $1,500,000 a year), he would say with complete equanimity: 'I guess I may be the first Astor to die insolvent.'

Newspaper-owning, penultimate infirmity of millionaire minds, had so far attracted only the English Astors (who had 'the other half' of the fortune). When William Waldorf Astor, 'Wealthy Willie', who was worth $80 million, decided in 1890 that 'America is not a fit place for a gentleman to live' and sought ways of penetrating the British aristocracy and satisfying his frustrated creative urge, he bought the *Pall Mall Gazette*. He reversed its political allegiance from Liberal to Conservative and then, because the editor would not let him write leading articles, founded two more periodicals, the *Pall Mall Magazine* and the *Pall Mall Budget*, and at last, in 1911, bought the *Observer* – not, however, with any idea of promoting social justice.

This was not Vincent's way. It seemed to him that *Time* magazine, with all its estimable qualities, did not give enough space to social theories and remedies for the Depression (it was now the 1930s). So he bought *Newsweek* with the idea that it should become an outlet for the ideas of Raymond C. Moley, one of President Roosevelt's academic Brains Trust. Roosevelt had become a close friend of Vincent's around 1921, when, stricken with polio, he had been told by his doctor to swim as much as possible, and Vincent had put at his disposal the swimming pool at Ferncliff, his 'bastard Dutch' mansion in a 3000-acre estate in Dutchess County, near Rhinebeck, beside the Hudson River only a few miles from Roosevelt's own Hyde Park. Roosevelt was also frequently a guest on Vincent's diesel yacht *Nourmahal* (several Astor yachts were named *Nourmahal*, which, with no significance that can be traced, seems to mean 'Light of the Harem').

We should not demand of the rich-rich that they devote the *whole* of their wealth to good causes. This is to destroy the worthwhileness of being rich-rich. In Vincent Astor's case, it was neither desirable nor necessary, since many of his pleasures added to the sum total of human knowledge as well as to the amusement of himself and his friends, who were generally people of achievement, be they university professors or prizefighters: they included, at various times, Cardinal Spellman, Moss Hart and Rex Harrison. We have already observed that great wealth enables people to realize their fantasies, especially childhood fantasies. 'Let's pretend' becomes 'dreams come true', and things one was forbidden to do in childhood turn into obsessions of adulthood. Fantasy things, beyond their imaginings, happen to fantasy-people who are unencumbered by poverty. All his life Vincent had been interested in aviation. He turned down what other members of his family would have given their right arms to have; a dukedom. For ex-King Manoel of Portugal offered to make him Commander-in-Chief of the Portuguese Air Force with the title, 'the Duke of Astor'.

It cannot be pretended that Vincent's practical jokes, so unamusing to their victims, were edifying. It gave him ungovernable joy to put iron sausages amid the bacon for his guests' breakfast; and among the pretzels there was sure to be one made of rubber. It really wasn't entirely pleasant to be Vincent's guest on the *Nourmahal*. If he knew where your money was invested, he would arrange bogus radio news bulletins announcing terrible falls in the stock market which could only mean your financial ruin. Franklin Roosevelt loved this sort of thing. One weekend at Ferncliff a guest arrived in the most luxurious new trailer caravan anyone had ever seen: it was a palace on wheels, filled with exquisite porcelain and calf-bound books. Mobilizing his servants to help, Vincent ringed it with bonfires soaked in paraffin and set them alight, so that the unhappy guest thought it had been destroyed by fire. And on a weekend house party at Newport, Rhode Island, he went to the trouble of having a special edition of a Sunday newspaper prepared, containing a scandalous story about one of his women guests, supplying copies not only to his guests but to all local newsagents ... It is one of those stories whose end is never known, and leaves one asking in frustration: were they ever on speaking terms again? Or did he just hate her anyway?

Juvenile, too, was the naïve spirit of adventure that ruled his cruises in the *Nourmahal*, which cost $1,750,000 to build and, with a crew of forty-two, $125,000 a year to run; it was skippered for years by a cheerful Swede, Captain Klang; and the crew included Vincent's two dachshunds, which accompanied him on all voyages. Vincent went to the Caribbean, to Iceland, to the South Pacific, where he loved to dive underwater and watch fishes. He sought out places where pirate treasure was said to be hidden – the Galapagos and Cocos Islands. He never found any, but it was fun looking; fun, above all, to be pursued by natives with garlands of flowers, to invite them aboard the yacht, and show them electric light, which none of them had ever seen before.

In the early 1930s there were persistent reports of people disappearing mysteriously on Charles Island in the Galapagos. One of them was a Mrs de Wagner, born in Vienna, who was said to call herself Queen of the Islands. This was exactly the sort of quest that Vincent loved, and in 1937 he sailed there to look for her. Another anticlimax: he never found her. What he found was a kind of penguin unique to the Galapagos. Among all the rich-rich we have studied, Vincent is the only penguin collector. He not only collected a great many live ones, which he gave away to various zoos, but there seemed to be a personal, perhaps symbolic bond between him and them. His custom-made cigarettes, of which he smoked fifty a day in addition to a foul-smelling corncob pipe, all had a penguin design on them. The radiator-cap of his 16-

cylinder Cadillac was a stainless steel penguin. He had penguin-shaped clocks, penguin bookends, penguin doorstops. Why did he love penguins so? 'Because they have feet like mine.'

Vincent was a great worrier; not, perhaps, about money; possibly about the state of the world; nobody knows for sure. But his remedy was a child's. He had, in the grounds at Ferncliff, a white marble copy of Marie Antoinette's Petit Trianon which his father had built: it had a swimming pool, squash courts, changing rooms. Here he could relax alone or with guests. He also, like Marie Antoinette, had a dairy farm where he seemed to find it soothing to watch cows being milked. But neither of these did him so much good as his model railways. He had two: one at Ferncliff, equipped with a snowplough for cold weather, the other at his Bermuda villa 'Ferry Reach', big enough to ride on with 850 feet of track. And when the Second World War broke out, Vincent went to his Bermuda railroad to think things over.

It was considered remarkable that Vincent could run three homes – Ferncliff, Ferry Reach and his modest (for an Astor) house at 130 East 80th Street – with only twenty servants. Of them all, one was totally indispensable: if the *Nourmahal* had capsized and he had been washed up on an uninhabited island, Vincent would have died without him – his valet. So dependent was he on that faithful Jeeves that when the man was ill, Vincent literally could not find his clothes. This made things very difficult for him when he was invited for the weekend to a house where there was no room for his valet. He would come down to breakfast barefoot because, he said, he 'couldn't get the damned trees out of the shoes.'

There was little stealth about the benefactions of the Guggenheims; but although they had had their share of anti-capitalist obloquy, it does not appear that anyone advised them to pour forth money to improve their 'image'. The generosity of Dan Guggenheim began impulsively: as soon as he heard about the San Francisco earthquake and fire on 18 April 1906, he sent $50,000 and a telegram: NO RED TAPE GIVE IT TO THE PEOPLE AT ONCE. The very method of distribution was emotional rather than practical. The money, in bills, was carried into the city by horse and cart. After this, the philanthropy of the Guggenheims followed, for the most part, their own inclinations – no bad way to give. 'The appalling Mrs Astor was dead,' says a chronicler of the family. 'The Social Register already counted for less. Jewish bankers like Otto Kahn were positively fashionable and were exposing the provincial backwardness of the gentile crust.' Old Meyer had exhausted himself amassing wealth: his children wanted to sweeten the sound and smell of the world. Thus Daniel and Florence provided $4 million, first to finance the popular Goldman concerts in Central Park, and eventually to build the Guggenheim Shell.

Most of the Guggenheims were culture-conscious, and some were race-conscious in that they sought to marry outside the family and into gentile English families. Only one, Daniel's son Meyer Robert, positively refused to work. 'Every family supports one gentleman of leisure,' he said when he was no more than twenty. 'I have elected to assume that position in mine.'

Daniel, who as early as 1906 had used the careful word 'socialistic' about his political views said: 'The money must go back to the people.' After the First World War he became fascinated by flying, the more so because a friend had been killed in an aircraft. It was not yet thought that flying would ever be a viable form of public transportation, and there was little money for research. Daniel and his son Harry started two funds for aeronautical research. Lindbergh's transatlantic flight in 1927 showed that they were on the right track. Captain James Doolittle's fog-landing and blind-flying experiments, aircraft safety devices, a gyroscopic compass, the pioneer Western Air Express airline, all were financed by Guggenheims. Chairs of aeronautical engineering were set up in several universities. A Hungarian space engineer, Theodor von Karman, inventor of the wind-tunnel, was brought over to the California Institute of Technology: to him can be traced the eventual success of the Douglas DC-3.

In his old age, in the late 1920s, Daniel Guggenheim heard of a 'mad professor' from Worcester, Massachusetts, who wanted to send rockets to the moon. This was Dr Robert H. Goddard, 'father of American rocketry'. Daniel transferred him to New Mexico, where there was more room than in his 'Aunt Effie's field' in Massachusetts. Here he developed a rocket called Nell which reached a height of 10,000 feet. Daniel did not really believe in moon exploration, but to a friend he said: 'I'm not going to live to see it, but you'll live to see the mail shot over to Europe.'

The interest of the Guggenheims in modern, not to say *avant-garde*, art seems to have begun with Solomon. Simon and his wife had in 1925 (in memory of their son John Simon, who had died of a mastoid infection when he was twenty-two) created a Foundation for annual fellowships 'to assist research and artistic creation', embracing writers, painters, musicians, scholars and scientists. No strings: anyone who

Left Twentieth-century
painters and sculptors owe
much to Peggy
Guggenheim; her palazzo
on the Grand Canal will
house them forever, 'even if
Venice sinks'. *Right* Peggy
Guggenheim in front of a
silver sculpture by
Alexander Calder.

seemed to need a year in which to develop something of value to himself
or humanity was eligible. Art patronage was continued by Solomon.
In 1926, when he was sixty-five, he met an improbable red-haired lady,
daughter of a German general, called Baroness Hilla von Rebay. She
took him to the Bauhaus, introduced him to Klee, Kandinsky and other
'non-objective' artists, and made him buy a lot of their pictures. One
artist, on whom she put nearly all her (or rather Solomon's) money,
Rudolf Bauer, turned out to be a plagiarist of Kandinsky, and his relationship with the Baroness ended in a fearful row, with Bauer accusing
her of being a Nazi agent.

The Baroness became the first director of the Solomon Guggenheim
Museum of Non-Objective Art which opened in 1939. It was born
in a storm of hostile criticism because the Baroness's own tastes were
so arbitrary – Dadaism and Surrealism, she said, were rubbish, and so
was Picasso. In the same atmosphere of controversy, Frank Lloyd

Wright's 'ziggurat' design for a building on 5th Avenue to house the collection was received with horror, which changed to a sort of pride during the fourteen years which elapsed between plans and completion. Peggy Guggenheim thought it looked like a huge multi-storey carpark.

We should, perhaps, rescue from oblivion Murry Guggenheim's free dental service for the poor of New York, which no longer exists but was a brave attempt at a health service. (The only parallel to it, on a much smaller scale, was perhaps Philip Sassoon's free dental clinic at his model workers' housing estate at East Cliffe, Folkestone.) The Guggenheims seem to have had trouble with their teeth; and it was probably a riding accident, resulting in the loss of several teeth, that was the turning point in Peggy Guggenheim's life. Peggy (Marguerite) is one of the three daughters of Ben Guggenheim, one of the brothers who had drifted away from the family business and spent much time living it up in Paris. He, like J. J. Astor IV, had gone down on the *Titanic*, putting on full evening dress so as to die like a gentleman.

Peggy came into her money in 1919 when she was twenty-one. It was not a big fortune, as fortunes go, and, alone among Guggenheim women, she made more than she inherited – not by any conscious business acumen but because she found that, by having her kind of fun with her money, more eventually came back to her than she had invested. Regarding many of her uncles as 'peculiar if not mad', she broke away at an early age and lived in Europe. There had been an indeterminate period in New York, during which she had had her teeth fixed for $2000 and her nose remodelled for $1000. Why, after all this, she should have taken a job as a dentist's assistant at $2.35 a day is not easy to understand; but it was not for long, and soon she was helping her cousin Harold Loeb (he was a model for Robert Cohn in Hemingway's *The Sun Also Rises*) to run a radical bookshop. Harold, who 'knew them all' in expatriate American Paris, whetted her appetite for the studios of Europe. She read Bernard Berenson, and met Alfred Stieglitz the photographer-dealer-impresario, who showed her the first abstract painting she had ever seen, by Georgia O'Keeffe.

In Europe she met the Surrealist Yves Tanguy, Brancusi and other artists whom she began to collect; Samuel Beckett; a number of men who loved the artist's life but never actually produced anything; and Laurence Vail, a writer, generally described as 'a professional Bohemian', to whom she was married for seven years. Then, in the late 1930s, she moved to London and opened 'Guggenheim Jeune' where, with the help of Marcel Duchamp, she organized *avant-garde* exhibitions – of Kandinsky, John Tunnard, Tanguy. (She observed various painters' attitudes towards money: Kandinsky was 'as businesslike as a stockbroker'; Tanguy, when he had sold a number of pictures, sat in cafés flicking screwed-up £1 notes to people at other tables.)

'Guggenheim Jeune' lost $6000 a year, and Peggy reckoned that she was also giving away about $10,000 a year to artists and hard-up friends. Undismayed, she planned a museum of modern art for London (the Tate Gallery was, she felt, obstructively conservative). It was to be directed by Herbert Read, then editing the *Burlington Magazine*. This was in 1939. When war was declared, Peggy, who seldom foresaw anything, simply moved to Paris, rented a shop in the Place Vendôme and stocked up by buying a picture a day. Three days before the Germans entered Paris, she packed up her pictures and fled south-east into what was then unoccupied France and hid them in Grenoble. America was not yet in the war, and she now began planning an artists' colony in the South of France.

But she had meanwhile met Max Ernst, who had suffered in concentration camps, and it seemed more important to get Jewish artists out of Europe than to risk letting them stay. With Ernst, her children by Laurence Vail and her pictures, she escaped to New York through Lisbon. Within a year she had started another gallery, 'Art of this Century', at 30 West 57th Street. In its very first exhibition she showed three new painters who have survived – William Baziotes, Robert Motherwell and Jackson Pollock. As the Baroness von Rebay had put all her money on Bauer, so Peggy Guggenheim put most of hers on Pollock, the first splash-drip 'action painter', for whom the contemporary description was 'abstract expressionist', and whom she called 'the greatest painter since Picasso'. And here she showed a shrewd business sense, for she locked him up in a contract by which he had to deliver all his output to her. It ended in rows, litigation and Pollock's death.

'Art of this Century' lasted until 1947. Now Peggy, perhaps sick of the New York scene, did what men and women dream of doing: she settled in Venice, exhibited her collection at the 1948 Biennale, and at last found a permanent home for her pictures at the Palazzo Venier dei Leoni, white and vine-covered and magical. Still restlessly she travelled, in Ceylon, India, the Mediterranean, Mexico. She never wavered in her belief that the discovery of Jackson Pollock 'alone justifies my effort'. She has willed her palazzo and collection to her Uncle Solomon's garage-like museum on 5th Avenue, on condition that it stays forever in Venice 'even if Venice sinks'.

14

GREEK BEATS GREEK

Colocotronis, Georgiades, Goulandris, Kulu-
kundis, Lemos, Lyras – obviously all Greeks, but who are they? If you
have no connection with Greece, shipping or the City of London, you
may never have heard of them. Their offices are nearly all in half a
square mile of the City, with solid addresses like Minories, London
Wall, St Mary Axe, Fenchurch Street, Leadenhall Street. Their private
addresses, with one or two notable exceptions, are in high-priced dis-
tricts such as Park Lane, Eaton Square, and that haunt of millionaires
(so frequently burgled that you have to have bars and locking devices
on all windows), Avenue Road, NW8. But in only a few cases do their
owners regard them as home. One of the dreams which the rich-rich
cherish – it has something in common with the desire to own and live
on a yacht – is to live on an island, preferably one you have bought.
In the case of many rich-rich Greeks, they have an unfair advantage:
they were born and raised on islands. You might think that this would
give them a hankering after solid land-masses; but no – once an islander,
always an islander, even if it's only the Isle of Wight. Such a person
is known (but only in very large dictionaries) as a *nesophile*: it is of
course from the Greek. One of the most prominent British nesophiles
was the late Sir Compton Mackenzie, who at various times owned two
of the Outer Hebrides and two of the tinier Channel Islands, Herm
and Jethou.

The best-known Greeks of all – Onassis, Niarchos, Livanos – are not listed above. It is because they *are* so well-known that other rich-rich Greeks are rather sniffy about them. They have got themselves bad publicity; they have broken the Greek code of manners which insists on secrecy and on all linen being washed in private. By all means have your children educated in Europe: the Colocotronis family favours Westminster School and St Edmund Hall, Oxford, which has also had two of the Georgiades family among its alumni (the two families are anyway connected by kinship and business). But do not marry the wrong kind of foreigner, and do not fly about the world telling people what the décor of your new yacht looks like, or how much money you have – it only attracts attention. We know that Stavros Livanos, described by his friends as 'a frugal sea-captain', when he died in 1963 left at least £100 million; but how much more we cannot tell, because wills and certain statistics are not available for publication in Greece.

Between Chios and the coast of Turkey, so close that either of them is almost within wading distance, lies the island of Oinousa, about seven miles along. Here live a little under 1600 people, among them fifty families with fortunes of at least £1 million each, of whom twenty are shipowners. Most of the island's roads, housing and schools have been built by the feudally munificent shipowning families. Strovili Lemos, who has a £75,000 house in Winnington Road, near Hampstead Golf Club, NW London, has a swimming pool that will always remind him of his origins: it is shaped like Oinousa. The rest of the house is, for a millionaire, modest: seven bedrooms, five marble bathrooms and a private chapel. He has another estate, Warren Hill House, at Newmarket where he keeps racehorses.

From the village of Kardamila, on Chios itself, come the Livanos family, whose most famous member was Tina, who married Aristotle Onassis (twenty-one years her senior) but left him in 1959 because of his internationally publicized affair with Maria Callas. Two years later she married the Marquess of Blandford. Her sister Eugenie married Onassis' deadly rival Stavros Niarchos, which made the two rivals brothers-in-law. The Livanos family, more united than most, was by no means split asunder: the two sisters stuck together, seeing each other, often without their husbands, either at St Moritz, where they went for winter sports, or in Paris, where both had luxury apartments.

What set Onassis and Niarchos apart from other Greek shipowners, and made them almost non-U to the others, was the fact that neither of them was born on an island. For Onassis, who had been born in

The wives of Stavros Niarchos: *left* Tina, *below* her sister Eugenie, *right* Charlotte Ford.

Smyrna, certain Greek islands had a romantic-cum-intellectual appeal. There is evidence that, had his youth not been upset by the Greco-Turkish War of 1922, he might have broken away from the family tobacco business, or at least postponed his business career, by going to Oxford to read classics. Instead, he found himself, before the age of twenty, on an Italian emigrant ship, the *Tomasso di Savoia*, 8000 tons, sailing to Buenos Aires. He did not remember much about the voyage, but one vision stayed in his mind shortly after the ship left Genoa: the brilliant lights of Monte Carlo, which he was one day to add to his business (and pleasure) interests.

In Buenos Aires he became a night telephonist at the British-owned United River Plate Telegraph Co, where he could use at least some of the five foreign languages in which he was reasonably fluent – Turkish, Spanish, English, Italian and Swedish. From this he returned to the trade of his ancestors, importing Balkan tobacco into Argentina, multiplying by six the amount hitherto imported. Then the buying of ships, the realization that carrying oil was 'the most exclusive club', the foresight that tankers would grow bigger and bigger. Like all the Greek names in the City of London, he had discovered what can be legitimately done under United States, Panamanian and Liberian flags, and the fact that a kind Labour Government in post-war Britain was, by a loophole that nobody for some years detected, offering money to non-British shipowners to build and operate their own ships abroad, supposedly in the interests of British exporters. In 1945 Onassis built the 45,000-ton *Tina Onassis*, then the largest tanker in the world, following it nine years later with the 47,000-ton *King Saud I*.

He seemingly enjoyed trouble – with the US Government because he had bought surplus ships from them without being an American citizen; with the Peruvian Government because the whaling fleet he had bought in 1948 had been bombed by Peruvian planes for entering their 200-mile Pacific offshore limit. He quickly sold the whole fleet to Japan, confiding to an interviewer: 'Oh, what fun that was!'

There was nothing in Onassis of the grinding nineteenth-century

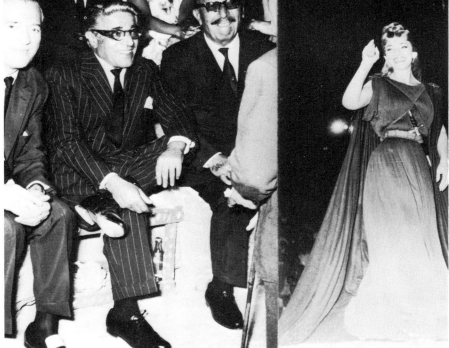

Onassis in his Callas phase. *Left:* he is in the front row for her appearance in Bellini's *Norma* in Athens. *Right:* she acknowledges the audience's ovation.

shipping tycoon. His ships were eminently seaworthy, and he spent lavishly on making life comfortable for his crews. 'Poverty drives men to sea,' he said; therefore living standards at sea must approximate to those ashore. Thus his very first tanker, *Ariston*, had one shower for every two men, a swimming pool and (for officers only) a grand piano.

Of all the Greek shipowners, Onassis alone diversified so widely. In the early 1950s he began what have been called his 'hobby enterprises'. Most Greek shipowners have few hobbies beyond the stereotyped ones: collecting art, for one reason or another; buying houses, buying and running racehorses. (The occasional flea-collector would be such a welcome break.) If, for Onassis, 'fun' was 'business' for far too long in his life, that is the way he was. The distant lights of Monte Carlo drew nearer as he acquired majority interests in the Sea Bathing Society, which is the famous Casino; five hotels, the opera house, its ballet company, a bathing beach and a hefty amount of real estate. It pleased the Prince of Monaco, who wished to attract more tourists, especially in the winter; and it pleased Onassis, who found Monte Carlo in many ways a better centre for his life than Athens.

He had also moved into airways and Greek tourism, acquiring in 1954 a twenty-year lease from the Greek Government to run Olympic Airways; and five years later he bought two luxury ships, the *Achilles* and *Agamemnon*. He had also done what all rich-rich men must do – he had bought a yacht. And what a yacht! Not exactly a refuge from the world's ignoble strife, since from the *Christina* he was in touch by radio telephone with anywhere in the world. The *Christina*, 1700 tons, was generally moored in Monte Carlo harbour, and Onassis lived on board when he was not in his apartment in the town. His most publicized cruise was in 1959, when he had among a small and select party of guests both Maria Callas and Sir Winston Churchill. They called, of course, at Ithaca, where Onassis could use his deep Homeric scholarship to instruct his guests. The *Christina* had ten guest rooms and forty crew. One room was Onassis's library: he specialized in books about sea voyages and archaeology. There were models of ships of all ages, and mosaic decorations based on those found at Knossos. In the main saloon there were usually only two pictures: an El Greco, and a Winston Churchill. The latter was there because it gave him pleasure; but also, he said, to remind him, every day, that: 'We are deeply indebted to him for the system of life which we enjoy, and to which he has given an extension of life.' That statement contains a wistful pessimism often to be found in rich men: it is of a piece with Gordon Selfridge saying:

'There will be no democracies in a hundred or two hundred years.'

'Some people seem to be ashamed of being millionaires. I'm not – why should I be?' The speaker is not Onassis, but Basil Mavroleon, who, being roughly the same age as the century, believed, as many still believed in the 1920s and 1930s, that it was the duty of rich-rich men to spend because by spending they would create employment, especially in the shipyards. Mavroleon had formed this opinion by 'seeing for himself' – not as thoroughly as George Orwell, but he had deliberately chosen to lodge with a taxi-driver's family in Brixton, South London, while learning the shipping business as a trainee with Kulukundis. Kulukundis, however, was unable to teach him the economics of running a luxury yacht. Yachts often appreciate in value and may therefore be regarded as investments: the danger lies in the upkeep. And when you are already running a racing stable and a stud farm, then your pleasures turn themselves into a business, which is all right if your business is also a recreation.

Mavroleon's first yacht, *Radiant I*, was bought from Lord Iliffe for £25,000 – dirt cheap, as luxury yachts go. He spent about £200,000 on it and eventually sold it to Kwame Nkrumah, who had recently become President of the Republic of Ghana, for £300,000. So far, so profitable. But he now began building *Radiant II* to his own designs, a 600-ton beauty with six double bedrooms, each with its own bathroom. In his own room he slept in a copy of Napoleon's bed. With a crew of twenty-four, *Radiant II* cost £50,000 a year to run. It became uneconomic, and Mavroleon sold it to another Greek shipowner for £600,000.

Not many children of shipowners escape the destiny of going into the family business, but one did: Elias Kulukundis, known to his friends as Eddie. Perhaps frustrated-creative himself, he told an interviewer that he 'knew no one to whom I could give money.' He took a calculated risk, and decided that the theatre was in need of his help. He set up as an independent producer in the early 1970s, and chose his younger dramatists well: Arnold Wesker, David Mercer and others who have since added television scripts to their work in the theatre.

But any consideration of great Greek spenders comes down to two, Onassis and Niarchos; and the pity of it is that, unless their furious rivalry gave them pleasure, it may have spoilt them as rich-rich figureheads. In business and pleasure they were very different. In business Onassis gathered well-trained down-to-earth (or down-to-water) Greeks around him; Niarchos liked well-born men of various European countries. The friends and guests of Niarchos tended to be people of birth and title, even royalty; those of Onassis were mostly people who had *done* something, in no matter what sphere – hence Churchill and Callas on the same cruise. As time went on, they seemed to be raiding each other's guests in a way which, for Onassis at least, was almost out of character.

In the matter of islands, we have seen that the frustration of Onassis's life was that he could not own Ithaca, could not be its twentieth-century Odysseus. Still, he could lavish love and gifts upon its 5800 people. There may have been a nagging doubt in his mind whether this really was Homer's Ithaca, since the *Odyssey* tells us that: 'Ithaca lies low, farthest up the sea line towards the darkness, but those other islands face the dawning and the sun,' which sounds much more like the larger island of Levkas, lying to the north. So it was perhaps in a mood of compromise that he finally decided on Skorpios, an uninhabited island, barely two miles long, only ten miles north of Ithaca. It was not an ideal choice, since Skorpios has very little drinking water – it has to import it all from Levkas; but Onassis made a harbour for the *Christina*, built a villa with subsidiary chalets in the grounds for his guests, and constructed three miles of roads. He planted olive groves; and having revived the life of the island with people most of whom worked for him, he built a telephone exchange. All this cost him £3 million.

One satisfaction of owning a Greek island is that you get such a lot of coastline for your money. An aerial view of Skorpios, two miles long, taken just before Onassis's wedding to Jacqueline Kennedy.

Niarchos's island was in a different part of Greece, within easy commuting distance of Piraeus. It was even smaller than Skorpios, only 240 acres, and its name was Spetsopoula. Here he too built a villa with fifteen rooms and a dozen chalets for guests; and for his shooting guests he stocked the tiny island with pheasants.

Niarchos had the Greek 'national' shipping line, Hellenic Shipyards: Onassis had the Greek 'national' airline, Olympic. When Onassis was centred on Monte Carlo, Niarchos was centred on London's Mayfair and his large chalet at St Moritz. Onassis chose pictures one by one; Niarchos collected Old Masters and French Impressionists with a kind of impatient greed – though perhaps the chance of buying Edward G. Robinson's collection of French Impressionists all at once was too good to miss.

The yacht life of Stavros Niarchos was less consistent than Onassis's. At the end of the Second World War he had a boat, made largely of ebony, named *Eros*, which he lent to Cole Porter in May 1946 for a two-week cruise among the Greek islands – 'this incredible gift from Stavros,' Cole wrote excitedly in his diary. The *Eros* was also lent, at times, to Elsa Maxwell: in return, Niarchos used to hint that his guests might like to contribute a few thousand dollars to his favourite charity, which was the Greek Archdiocese of North and South America. Later, Niarchos had a sailing yacht called *Creole*, whose cabins were panelled in oak and whose walls had been decorated by Salvador Dali.

In the summer of 1959, public attention – by which we mean press photography – was concentrated on the Riviera. Onassis had rented the Château de la Croë on Cap d'Antibes, where the Duke and Duchess of Windsor had lived just before the War. In Cannes harbour was the *Shemara*, owned by Sir Bernard and Lady Docker – a large white yacht which was one of the two things the average reader (and average shareholder) knew about both the Dockers and the Midland industry that provided their wealth, to wit, the BSA Company, which made small arms, motorcycles and various other useful things like nuts and bolts. The other thing they knew was that the Dockers owned a gold-plated Daimler automobile. These would excite little comment today; but the Dockers were not pop-stars, and in 1959 it was Going Too Far. The Dockers, whose lifestyle was overindulgent in other ways too, obstinately maintained that they were promoting, by bringing glamour to, the company's products.

Farther west, the still genuinely Bohemian old port of St Tropez,

Jackie and Ari on Skorpios.

its prices not yet inflated, its fashionableness still restricted to a comparative minority, was being discovered by Americans such as Henry Ford II and his daughters Charlotte and Anne, who had recently been guests of the Dockers on board the *Shemara*. Charlotte had just met young George Livanos, son of the shipowner. These two drove together to the Château de la Croë, where they found that their host, Onassis, could be their host for only a very short time. Onassis had rented the château, but Niarchos had *bought* it and wanted immediate possession. Further complications: Niarchos fell in love with Charlotte, who was thirty-two years younger, wooed her with a $\$\frac{1}{2}$ million engagement ring, divorced his third wife Eugenie, and married Charlotte. The marriage lasted a little over a year. In the final analysis, the oneupmanship was Onassis's: he married the widow of the most glamorous American President, and stayed married to her until his death. To have beaten that, Niarchos would have had to marry the Queen of England.

It was a strange marriage indeed. Did they get His 'n Her money's worth? Onassis gave his wife three million dollars, a million for each of her children, an income of $480,000 a year, and, as a wedding present, a ring, with matching earrings, valued at over a million dollars. The day after they were married on Skorpios in 1968 he flew to Athens on business. Perhaps business was after all his true love – the only thing that could revive his youthful exhilaration after overcoming an enemy or an obstacle – 'Oh, what fun that was!'

177

THE RICH ARE ALWAYS WITH US

 *P*aul Getty's father used to tell him: 'Never talk to people about money. You will always find it embarrassing because they will never have so much as you have.' But that was more than sixty years ago, when people of widely differing means led widely differing lives. Goronwy Rees, in a perceptive survey of six multi-millionaires some years ago, bridged the remaining gap by suggesting that (as Dorothy Parker said of Jews) the rich-rich are 'just like other people only more so': at last a challenge to the received opinion of Scott Fitzgerald and Hemingway that the rich are *different*. If they get rich-rich very suddenly, people feel obliged to do the things rich-rich people do, such as owning large yachts, which they seldom have time to use, or doing this racehorse-owning thing, or this Marbella-villa-owning thing, or this gambling-at-the-Clermont thing; above all, this living-in-a-tax-haven thing.

In the good old days (before 1900) the rich-rich spent spectacularly because there was little or no income tax and no death duties. Now their declining numbers spend (at least in the oil-consuming countries) because there *are* taxes: they spend tax-deductibly. Yet it is believed (though no one can prove it) that in Britain there are today no personal fortunes greater than £50 million ($85 million). And in 1966 a study of four hundred Americans with incomes of $1 million or more showed that one third of them did not work, or at least declared no earned income; and that most of the remaining two thirds got only three per

At a party on her 40th birthday Liz Taylor wears a present from husband Richard Burton – a £380,000 diamond pendant.

cent of their income by working. So there are theoretically still a surprising number of Americans (and possibly even one or two British) who have nothing to do but spend. Long may this continue, so long as it gives them and their friends pleasure.

Some of the tax-havens are closing down. About nine thousand houses and flats in the Swiss canton of Ticino stand empty since 1 January 1977, when new local tax laws made it no longer so attractive for foreign businessmen, film stars and best-selling authors to establish an official residence in Ascona, Locarno or Lugano. Prominent among them is Baron Heini von Thyssen-Bornemisza, grandson of the *Schlotbaron* August Thyssen, founder of a Ruhr steel dynasty; he has however left his villa open to the public so that they can see his priceless collection of Holbeins, Dutch masters, El Grecos and Titians.

Who are the international rich-rich today? Among the inheritors who have not buried their talents are the Thyssens and Flicks in Germany, the Peugeots in France, the Pearsons and Vesteys in Britain, the Agnellis and Pirellis in Italy, the Rockefellers in the United States. But where does all the opulence go? Were it not for the gossip writers, we should learn little about their manner of spending. Lord Cowdray, head of a financial empire which comprises Lazards' merchant bank, *The Financial Times*, seventy-three provincial newspapers, Penguin Books, oil companies in America and Canada, the Bordeaux vineyard of Château Latour and a lot of land in Scotland and Sussex, is a retiring man. It is his elder son, Michael Pearson, who makes the news: he inherited £7 million on his twenty-first birthday in 1966, has produced a few films, once owned a large yacht called *Hedonist*, and has recently announced his intention of living abroad until there is a change of government: 'Even at ninety-eight per cent, nobody would mind paying their taxes, as long as some use is being made of it.' His playboy image is almost Texan: he likes to wear cowboy boots and Stetson hats.

Goldsmith, the Anglo-French food and finance King, Slater, the asset-stripping whizz kind, Harry Hyams – post-war millionaires all – do most of the usual things millionaires do, and there is a touch of the glorious past in the fact that property-dealer Hyams, owner of the Centre Point office block in London, is also the owner of the Dockers' 878-ton yacht *Shemara*. For the true rich-rich eccentricity we must turn to Hollywood and the pop music scene. It is reckoned that Keith Moon of The Who pop group has paid out about £200,000 for the pleasure of wrecking hotel rooms, not excluding the Beverly Wilshire, Los Angeles. And something of the old Hollywood lives on in Sammy

Davis Jr, whose home in Beverly Hills – we could guess its cost at about $1 million – is modest in size (only twenty-five rooms, including a film library of a thousand features and tapes and a bar full of photographs of Sammy with friends and co-stars), with twenty-five television sets and only five cars (two Stutz Blackhawks, said to have cost $50,000 each, a $100,000 Rolls bought, sight unseen, after looking at an 'artist's impression' of it, a Thunderbird, and another car like yours or mine). Among many electronic gadgets is a system of room-to-room speakers. Sammy's staff of seventeen costs him $30,000 a week. He has been known to give luncheon parties for more than sixty people at a time and then pick up a bill for $3000. There was a time when he used to give everyone or anyone a 350-dollar solid gold cigarette-lighter. Yet he still has a dream about his lifestyle: 'I want to have three of everything – houses, cars, clothes – the same lifestyle in three different places – no worry about suitcases...'

Sammy Davis Jr takes delivery of his new Rolls Royce Silver Shadow convertible at Heathrow Airport, London.

Only a dedicated leveller like the fiery Labour politician, Mr Michael Foot, on record as saying that no one, anywhere, should be allowed to have more than £5000 a year (with no mention of any adjustment for inflation), could believe that there will be no more new millionaires.

The late Paul Getty, stressing the importance of *thinking* like a million-aire, said in one of his two autobiographical books: 'Large fortunes will be made in the next two decades by men who are beginners today.' (He was not thinking of pop-stars, either.) And again: 'There are a hundred men seeking security to one able man who is willing to risk his fortune.' Let us hope that their spending will match the efforts of their accumulating energy. Future rich-rich men may come from the most unexpected quarters. There are a number of extremely rich men in the Soviet Union, often with the title of Commissar or Hero of Socialist Labour, who are privileged in ways which would, or should, earn Mr Foot's disapproval. The state may take a percentage of Aram Khatchaturian's 'Sabre Dance' and *Onedin Line* royalties which he has collected in the West, but there will be plenty left to support his elegant Moscow apartment near the Conservatoire, his *dacha* in Snegiri, twenty-seven miles outside the capital, and the house in his native Armenia which was presented to him by the Soviet Government. He has two chauffeurs for his four cars (a Volga, a Zhiguli, a Buick and a Mercedes), two permanent guards on his *dacha*, and a staff of six who cost him $1200 a month. It may have been awareness of this trend in Soviet culture that inspired Cyrus S. Eaton, sometime office boy to John D. Rockefeller I and Cleveland, Ohio, investment banker, to befriend Kruschev and Mikoyan in the hope that there could after all be a working compromise between capitalism and communism.

Prosperous clergymen are an American speciality, from Father Divine onwards: the latest is Dr Frederick J. Eikerenkoetter II, known to his enormous flock as Reverend Ike. It is not immediately clear why the head of the United Christian Evangelistic Association should require sixteen Rolls-Royces and five homes, one on an almost inaccessible mountain top in California, one on a beach, one near the Hudson in New York State, one in Beverly Hills and a beautiful apartment in Manhattan. Gold rings adorn his fingers, a diamond watch his wrist. He is said to pay $800 for his suits. His church is a converted cinema in the old 1930s Moorish style (generally associated with Loews in America and Odeons in Britain), and his pulpit is a podium which rises out of the floor like a Wurlitzer organ. 'My salary ranges from $32,000 to $75,000 a year, but my church gives me very generous expenses,' he says. His church's wealth, which he augments by shrewd investment, is said to total some $17 million. He doesn't believe in kneeling for prayer – kneeling is simply an invitation to someone to kick you up the behind. 'You must love yourself before you can love anyone else.

Reverend 'Ike' Eikerenkoetter relaxes with a sip of milk during a
break in his preaching. The crown on the Chair represents the view
that 'there is a kingly Christ in every man'.

Success is always the theme.' Only sin stands in the way of self-im-
provement. How, the Reverend Ike is often asked, does he reconcile
his Rolls-Royces with the fact that Christ went barefoot? 'He rode on
the Rolls-Royce of his day, which was an ass.'

There are signs that the pattern of Arab spending is changing; that
the newly oil-rich Emirs and their entourages are losing the habit of
lavish ostentation and seeking true elegance; are investing their oil
profits in local industry and social services before the oil runs out. The
Reverend Ike is right: wealth is a good thing. By filling Arabia with
televisions, books, houses, furniture, golf courses, automobiles, air-conditioning and education, its rulers, whether they like it or not, are hurt-
ling towards the tearing aside of the veil and the emancipation of
women, far faster than it ever happened in the West. Any minute they
will discover taxation. As for education, consider this recent interview
between a Saudi Arabian parent and the headmaster of an English
public school. The headmaster offered to show him round the school.
'That is not necessary,' said the father. 'My son is very spoiled. He has
his own car and everything. I want him to come to your school and

sleep in your cold dormitories and catch nasty colds like all your other pupils.'

So let us look at the bonanza while it is still here. At the 1976 London Motor Show eighteen oil sheikhs ordered the new 140 mph Aston-Martin Lagonda, price £24,500, before it was even in production, thus pulling the company out of the red. One of the buyers was Sheikh Taufiq Aziz of Qatar, who bought three. Another three were ordered by an Oxford undergraduate, Rafih Abdul Aziz of Saudi Arabia. There are about four thousand people in the world who can afford 'supercars' and about a quarter of them are from Arabia.

Buying up hotels and West End apartments, the London Arab population increases. The Emir of Kuwait paid over £1 million for a house called 'Fairview' at Beaconsfield, Buckinghamshire, set in ninety acres, with two swimming pools, a cinema and a private telephone exchange. Those who come to enjoy themselves do so largely because there is so little to spend their money on at home. At the Omar Khayyam cabaret in Regent Street the belly-dancers writhe and the patrons stuff £5 and £10 notes into their exiguous pants, or drape them with chains of paper money like leis. At home gambling is forbidden by Muslim law, but at Ladbrokes' gaming tables the Governor of Riyadh lost £2 million in three nights and nonchalantly tipped the waiters with £100 chips. It has become fashionable to come to London for medical care and operations: the Kuwait Embassy has a 'health attaché' who is believed to have dealt with nearly a thousand willing patients in less than a year (no doubt the Omar Khayyam is part of the therapy). At £100 a day for a room at a fashionable clinic it is a bargain.

Crown Prince Fahd of Saudi Arabia, brother of King Khaled, whose private Jumbo jet 747 symbolizes the fact that he sits on twenty-three per cent of the world's known oil reserves, amused himself in September 1974 by trying to break the bank at Monte Carlo, but gave up after losing £5½ million.

However, Saudi Arabia has much healthier pursuits. Football, for example. Once a month Jimmy Hill, who once played for Fulham and is now reorganizing Saudi Arabian football, flies to Riyadh to train the local team. He has a five-year contract to spend £25 million on the task, which is closely supervised by Prince Faisal, King Khaled's brother and Minister for Sport, who cemented their friendship by giving Jimmy a watch with his, Faisal's, picture on the dial. One day they will play England, but for the moment nothing matters more than to be able to beat Kuwait.

Not since Barbara Hutton, granddaughter of F. W. Woolworth, celebrated her coming-out in 1932, at the nadir of the Depression, by having four orchestras and Rudy Vallee flown to her party (thus beating Doris Duke's in 1930 by one orchestra and a crooner), not since the Ringling Brothers' circus was hired by Evalyn Walsh McLean for little Vinson her son, had anyone staged such a birthday treat (for himself and officers of his Royal Police) as the Sultan of Oman did in November 1976. He imported a circus, Gerry Cottle's, whose normal habitat is Clapham Common, South-West London. The previous year he had sent for the Grenadier Guards, complete with band: His Majesty Sultan Qaboos bin Said, who was trained at Sandhurst, is a connoisseur of military display. But the logistics of crating and flying four Indian elephants (Brownie, Rebecca, Vicki and Geeta) weighing about $1\frac{1}{2}$ tons each, a fifteen-ton Big Top, 2500 seats for the audience, five lions, seven horses, four tons of straw, and all the acts (which included a strong man from Persia, a fire-eater, a motorcycle high-wire act, and clowns to throw buckets of water over each other) were worth the £150,000 fee to all concerned.

The lifestyle of Adnan Mohamed Khashoggi, 'the Onassis of Saudi Arabia', repays study. He is head of the multinational £400 million Triad Holding Corporation, which embraces cargo ships, armaments, banks and much else besides. He is now said to be worth £200 million. His career has been, not rags to riches, but silk robes to rich-riches. Part of his education was in California, where he invested a gift of $10,000 from his father (who was one of King Ibn Saud's private doctors) in a truck rental business. He is not only the boss of Triad, he is also its principal salesman. Most of his life centres on the personal Boeing 727 in which he commutes between the thirty-five or so countries where his customers – and potential customers – are. The plane, fitted up like a luxury apartment-cum-office with wall-to-wall carpets and a 40-ft sitting room, was bought for £6 million and costs £350,000 a year to run. The bedroom has two wardrobes, one full of Savile Row suits for Western countries, the other full of gold-embellished robes for the East. I have been unable to check reports that the lavatory seats are gold-plated: if so, I hope they are electrically warmed. He has besides one or two other smaller jets.

He is also building a 350-ft yacht with six guest suites, a system by which he can use satellite radio to talk to anywhere in the world, and a helicopter deck. This he will add to his two other yachts, the 500-ton *Mohamedia* (His) and the 380-ton *Khalidia* (mainly Hers, i.e. his wife

Soraya's), both with cinemas on board. With nearly a dozen homes in London, France, America, Italy, Marbella and several Arab states, and the Seychelles where he recently bought an eighty-five-acre estate beside Beau Vallon Bay ('the most beautiful beach in the world') on the island of Mahé, he is the one contemporary tycoon who comes near to, if he does not surpass, the Dinosaurs of the golden age of big spenders.

Khashoggi is thus in a position, by one form of transport or another, to be anywhere he likes in the world at a moment's notice. Christmas and New Year (Christian, not Muslim) 1976 found him at Gstaad, and this is the link between him and the Jet Set, of which he, more than anyone, is a rightful member.

There was a period just after the Second World War when it seemed that there were no new rich-rich; or that if there were, there wasn't enough opportunity to spend in a news-making way. The children of the same old rich-rich families made occasional headlines. Horace Dodge Jr, of the automobile dynasty, whose parents had once been 'King and Queen of Palm Beach Society', rubbing along on an income of only $25,000 a year, had been married four times before he met his Waterloo in 1952 and got engaged to her. She was a TV actress named Gregg Sherwood, and at twenty-seven she was exactly half his age. The engagement party was held, not in Horace's stately home St Leonard's (103 rooms), on the edge of Windsor Great Park, but in the Palm Beach Casino at Cannes, the family and guests being accommodated at an hotel where suites cost $200 a day. There were trips to Switzerland in a chartered aircraft at $1000 a time, and fifty guests were brought, also in chartered planes, from London, Paris and Rome. There was a touch of true old-world spending in the half-hundredweight of caviare (at $5 an ounce) especially flown from Astrakhan, the 1700 dozen roses, the thousand giant orchids at $15 each, and the gifts of scent and cigarette-holders to all the guests. Gregg's ring cost $100,000.

A little mental arithmetic quickly demonstrates that all this was somewhat in excess of Horace's means. Some bills, perhaps most bills, had not yet been paid. It then appeared that his fourth wife Clara Mae was demanding a $3 million divorce settlement. Gregg wrote some newspaper articles about poor Horace, and eventually, being at heart a kind girl, founded a 'home for lost girls' at Palm Beach, Florida.

The compulsive house-buying, and frequent husband-changing (nearly always to their financial cost), of Doris Duke and Barbara Hutton fascinated gossip-writers through the 1940s and 1950s: they had in common, apart from a great deal of money, the fact that each, at an interval of five years, was married to a musical-comedy character named Porfirio Rubirosa, sometime chargé d'affaires in Paris for the Dominican Republic. Barbara's union with him lasted only seventy-two days.

London's favourite millionaire at this time, a really *jolly* millionaire and a true eccentric, was Nubar Gulbenkian. He was everything his withdrawn, fundamentally mean father Calouste was not. Living mostly in a £20-a-day suite at the Ritz (which his father had provided the finance to build in 1906), he was noted for his extraordinary willingness to come to anyone's party. As such, he was a gift to publicity organizers, who knew that if Nubar were present their product was certain to be mentioned in gossip columns. He would arrive in his old-fashioned chauffeur-driven taxi, which was so tall that he could sit in it without taking his top-hat off (there is a parallel in New York's Willie Walter, a financier who believed that his glaucoma had been caused by bumping his head on the roof of his car, and so had designed for

Nubar Gulbenkian in his famous taxi-cab: 'It turns on a sixpence, whatever that is.'

himself a Pierce-Arrow tall enough for him to stand upright in).

Nubar's little joke about his taxi was: 'They tell me it turns on a sixpence, whatever that is.' His theatrical bonhomie, the invariable orchid in his buttonhole, his blue-rinsed beard, his love of riding to hounds ('I bet you've never seen an Armenian hunting before!'), the hours he spent with manicurists, were all one great protest against his father's way of life. The hunting had been a sore point with old Calouste since the First World War, when Nubar was at Cambridge: 'I sent you to be educated, not to kill yourself.' Would the boy never grow up? No, he would not. In 1940, aged forty-four, Nubar actually sued his father for five per cent of Calouste's famous five per cent; and in 1953, two years before his death, Calouste altered his will so that Nubar was cut off with a mere million pounds, plus £1½ million in trust.

In July 1962 the cover of *Vogue* (American edition) carried a headline: 'What the Beautiful People Are Doing this Summer'. *Vogue* had coined this expression to describe a new class of free spenders, not rich in the Vanderbilt sense, but rushing about the world as if it were going to end next year. Nearly all of them were self-made and relatively class-less; different from the classical rich-rich in that those who made the money are spending it *now*, with no attempt to erect memorials to themselves. *Vogue* described them as 'good-looking people doing fun-things', and raised an eyebrow at 'the offhand way people race off to Tanganyika, Kyoto, Afghanistan, as casually as they do to the Greek Islands, the Côte d'Azur, the Costa Brava and the Skaggerak'.

At about the same time (perhaps a little before) Igor Cassini, better known as Cholly Knickerbocker the columnist, used the phrase 'The Jet Set' to describe a new generation who regarded the 1950s as starchy and practically pre-war. It soon became clear that Cholly and *Vogue* were talking about the same people. They were cosmopolitan. They played backgammon. They reckoned to spend not less than £30,000 a year on travel, hotels and clothes. If they were women, they were sometimes *lent* clothes by couturiers for publicity purposes. Their hair was done (every day) by Vidal Sassoon or Alexandre. They frequented Régine's in Paris, holidayed at Acapulco, had villas at Lyford Cay, Bahamas, spent Christmas and New Year at Gstaad (already we are beginning to speak of them in the past tense). At one end of the scale were the Windsors, certain Fords and Greeks, Jacqueline Kennedy (afterwards known to the New York *Women's Wear Daily* as Jackie O, as the Beautiful People were abbreviated by them to BPs, like the gasoline); and Antenor Patino, the Bolivian tin man. These were the

Old Guard; and so to the other end of the gamut, in no particular order – Roger Vadim, Jane Birkin, Mick and Bianca Jagger, the Vicomtesssse de Ribes of high fashion, the omnipresent, sometimes topless symbol of the age, Marisa Berenson.

Gstaad and St Tropez, Gunther Sachs at St Moritz with his income of more than £2000 a day from the family car components business, Princess Ira Fürstenberg in Rome (can it be more than twenty years since she married, at the age of fifteen, her first playboy, Alfonso von Hohenlohe?). If you live in Marbella in Southern Spain you can go to Monte Carlo for your holidays and still meet the same people. One of them will be Princess Mary Obolensky, who organizes backgammon tournaments for the rich-rich. Another may well be Harold Robbins on his yacht in Cannes harbour. Should you find yourself stuck for conversation, and you didn't want to risk asking: 'Who do you think Fiona Thyssen is going to marry next?' it would be quite safe to say: 'Darling, I haven't seen you since Acapulco!'

At Ferrières, of course, you would have to say it in French. Not quite classifiable as Beautiful People, yet numbering many of them among their acquaintance, the French Rothschilds have kept the old rich-rich tradition of fancy dress balls going. A turning point was reached in 1972, when Baroness Marie-Hélène de Rothschild, second wife of Baron Guy, gave a Surrealist ball. Brigitte Bardot had her hair dressed by a Surrealist painter named Leonor Fini. Bettina, model-girl friend of the late Aly Khan, had a headdress which created the illusion of a dagger through her skull, complete with rubies, representing blood, cascading down one cheek. The wife of the chairman of a large department store danced with her head in a birdcage. Against the Rothschild collection of Old Masters, a new décor by Salvador Dali clashed upsettingly. It was unfortunate that this brilliant entertainment took place at the height of a strike of garbage collectors, so that guests had to make their way to Ferrières through mountains of decaying refuse in the outer suburbs of Paris. Perhaps it was a warning; a second warning against the display of wealth – the first, four years before, had been the holding up for ransom of Guy's first wife Alix and their son David.

In Buckinghamshire, Baron Mayer's Mentmore Towers, with its £3 million art collection, was sold in May 1977 by its last owner, Lord Rosebery, to pay off £4½ million in death duties. Mrs E. T. Stotesbury's Whitemarsh Hall became a research laboratory for the Pennsylvania Salt Manufacturing Company. And Philip Sassoon's old house in Park

Lane is now the Playboy Club, which at least carries on the tradition of spending for pleasure.

To feel nostalgia for the golden age of the rich-rich is hardly permissible now. Freedom to spend is not one of the principles of the Atlantic Charter. Freedom to spend enabled James (Diamond Jim) Brady to consume, at one sitting, a twelve-course dinner (with several helpings of several courses), beginning with six dozen oysters and ending with five pounds of soft-centred chocolates: not competitively, but regularly; a feat which, were he alive today, would have made him eligible for the *Guinness Book of Records*. Freedom to spend enabled the 6th Duke of Devonshire to demolish the village of Edensor in Derbyshire simply because it spoilt one of the vistas from Chatsworth House; the same freedom enabled him to compensate the tenants with a brand-new model village. Freedom to spend enabled James Gordon Bennett, proprietor of two New York newspapers, to buy a Monte Carlo restaurant on the spot out of rage because he had not been given his usual table; and then, having finished his meal, to give the whole place to one of the waiters. Freedom to spend, or rather a temporary unconsciousness of being rich-rich, enabled Cole Porter to do the gentlemanly thing in the Ritz Bar, Paris, when Moss Hart brought him a gift of some gold sock-suspenders. Cole immediately put them on, and gave his old ones to the bartender: there was just time for Hart to notice that they too were of gold. Freedom to spend, to chuck away, to relax with that absence of anxiety which only the rich-rich know, dictated the reaction of Lucy Houston one day on the good ship *Liberty*, when, emptying garbage through a porthole, she realized that a piece of soiled cotton-wool contained £1200 worth of pearls. In a rare moment of self-criticism, she giggled: 'Oh, how stupid of me!'

In our study of the rich-rich, we are bound, if we are honest, to come to the conclusion that our interest in them is based on a bitter-sweet concoction of curiosity and envy. The Have-Nots envy the Haves, and the Haves envy the Have-Mores. Nothing will ever change this. It *is* possible to be both virtuous *and* have cakes and ale; only let us not be puritanical about money. And so let us end with a quotation from the late Toots Shor, the New York restaurateur, which has passed into folklore: 'I don't want to be a millionaire – I just want to live like one.'

Bibliography

Among many books consulted, the following were especially helpful:

Bainbridge, John, *The Super-Americans*
Batty, Peter. *The House of Krupp*
Beaton, Cecil, *The Wandering Years*
Beebe, Lucius, *The Big Spenders*
Birmingham, Stephen, *Our Crowd* and *Real Lace*
Clark, Kenneth, *Another Part of the Wood*
Collier, Peter and Horowitz, David, *The Rockefellers*
Collis Brown, Henry, *In the Golden Nineties*
Cowles, Virginia, *The Rothschilds*
French, Philip, *The Movie Moguls*
Frischauer, Willi, *Millionaires' Islands* and *The Aga Khans*
Goodwyn, Frank, *Lone-Star Land*
Guggenheim, Peggy, *Confessions of an Art Addict*
Head, Alice, *It Could Never Have Happened*
Heller, Robert, *The Common Millionaire*
Hewins, Ralph, *Mr. Five Per Cent*
Hoyt, Edwin P., *The Vanderbilts and their Fortunes*
Jackson, Stanley, *The Sassoons*
James, R. R. (ed.), *Chips: the Diary of Sir Henry Channon*
Kavaler, Lucy, *The Astors*
Kimball, Robert (ed.), *Cole*
Lilly, Doris, *Those Fabulous Greeks*
Lord, John, *The Maharajahs*
Lundberg, Ferdinand, *America's Sixty Families*
Maclean, Evalyn and Sparkes, Boyden, *Father Struck It Rich*
Manchester, William, *The Arms of Krupp*
Maxwell, Elsa, *The Celebrity Circus*
Morton, Frederic, *The Rothschilds*
Nichols, Beverley, *The Sweet and Twenties*
Penguin, *Profiles from The New Yorker*
Potocki, Alfred, *Master of Lançut*
Pound, Reginald, *Selfridge*
Rees, Goronwy, *The Multi-Millionaires*
Sitwell, Osbert, *Laughter in the Next Room* and *The Scarlet Tree*
Swanberg, W. A. *Citizen Hearst*
Tebbel, John, *The Inheritors*
Tolbert, Frank X., *Neiman-Marcus, Texas*
Vanderbilt, Gloria and Thelma Lady Furness, *Double Exposure*
Viner, Richard, *George of the Ritz*
von Klass, Gert, *Krupps: the Story of an Industrial Empire*
Waugh, Alec, *The Lipton Story*
Wentworth, Day, J., *Lady Houston, D.B.E.*
Williams, A. H., *No Name on the Door*
Wykes, Alan, *Gambling*

Index

192